Lit Up

Out of the cubicle and into the real world

Eddy Gilmore

This is a work of nonfiction.

Cover art by Shawna Gilmore
Designed by Naomi Christenson

ISBN: 979-8-9895531-0-5 (print)
ISBN: 979-8-9895531-1-2 (digital)

For Emma and Josiah.

Because the events that follow only made you stronger.

For images, visit www.EddyGilmore.com/lit-up-photos/
password "Lit"

Act I

You can't think yourself out of a cubicle.

1

Rising carefully with headset connected via cord to network, I peered across an ocean of identical gray cubicles. Amidst a low hum of activity, one thousand employees clad in corporate casual bore vacant expressions. Eyes fixed upon glowing monitors. Keyboards clicked.

Two guppies swam the fishbowl atop my desk. My life seemed similar. Direct deposits, every other week, were like sprinkles of fish food to keep me going. Not too much now! Just a pinch. Enough to pay basic bills.

I circumnavigated the outer edges of this cosmos during breaks. Strolling the parking lots ringing the large rectangle, I cut across small bits of grass. Pine cones crunched underfoot. A tenuous connection to the material world, it felt real.

After pounding pavement became unsatisfying, I adventured into the adjoining woods. The challenge became returning to my desk on time without consulting a watch, in 15 minutes by instinct alone. Pristine shoes collected traces of mud, evidence of connection to the organic universe. Mushrooms across the color spectrum attracted my attention. I dropped to all fours while gazing into the mysterious realm of Kingdom Fungi. I was desperate for encounters with the wild and uncontrollable, an alternative dimension to the pixelated world inside the computer.

Journeys carried me through the brush beside Snowflake Nordic Center, which was operated by George Hovland, a veteran of the 1952 Winter Olympics. I glimpsed his shock of white hair investigating my entry point into the woods in late fall, after stomping through the first three inches of snow. The next day, instead of a simple No Trespassing sign, an impressive wall of logs and brush had materialized, apparently designed to keep out hordes of nature-starved barbarians. I imagine him fretting about a cubicle-zombie apocalypse: hundreds of bloated, chain-smoking, chair-sitters overwhelming his ski trails. He was in his 80s, and this Great Wall was eight feet high! All for little old me, this testifies to his boundless energy spent promoting and protecting the sport of cross-country skiing, the stuff of legend. Apologies, kind sir.

The material world shrank even further when connection to The Matrix came through a tiny office beneath my home. While sitting at this portal, six inches passed between me and the cold stone wall. A room designed to hold coal for heating the house, the space measured 4' X 5', half the size of The Hole in Alcatraz. A view out the window was at grass height.

No taskmaster or lock held me there. A deluge of emails kept me chained to the desk. I missed the 12-mile commute by bicycle, but the convenience of hopping into my chair and firing up the boilers in pajamas was bewitching. The ease of the arrangement, spiritual and emotional turmoil notwithstanding, heaped another half-decade onto my sentence. I latched onto this life-sustaining corporate teat like a helpless babe for 12 soul-sucking years.

The atmosphere was thick with loneliness. Co-workers were hundreds of miles away, sitting in home offices at opposite ends of the country. In solitary confinement, corner-occupying spiders became companions. Death-defying descents from the ceiling in free fall produced a shot of adrenaline when they suddenly appeared between face and screen, bouncing at the end of a bungee cord. This was the signal to clear the room. The cell—18-inch-thick rock walls festooned with cobwebs above, beside, and beneath—had become fit for the Addams Family. Welcome mat laid out, new friends migrated in. The cycle repeated itself every six months.

The company's relationship with the Grim Reaper, who combed through every nook and cranny of the organization about twice each year, proceeded similarly. A terrifying brush with destiny, we all knew it might be our own heads on the chopping block one day. I was deluded that it'd never happen to me. I knew far too much, and was vital for day-to-day operations, peon though I was. The company's stock rocketed to new heights after my departure. I lost track at 400% higher. Every cog is replaceable in a machine. There are no exceptions.

Predictably, when least expected, I joined a conference call with a complete stranger that changed my family's life forever. The greatest injustice is that I didn't initiate this call myself, years earlier.

2

She severed our relationship in one quick motion. That was the icebreaker. Bargaining and pleading were ineffectual. A bean-counter had manipulated a spreadsheet, deleting a single line item. Stunned by the realization of a sealed fate on an otherwise ordinary morning, floodgates opened. Tears poured out of me in an unending torrent.

Surplus emotion on my side of the chasm.

Cold and clinical on theirs. Just another Tuesday.

"It's not personal. It's business."

An asymmetrical, tectonic event.

My family had no other income to depend upon, and no

prospects. My complete failure in preparing for this inevitable outcome was most upsetting of all. The company had a long track record of laying off amazing people throughout my tenure, thus compounding the foolishness of placing all of our financial eggs into this single basket.

Ten minutes after being sacked, I sped out of town atop my bicycle. It was the only appropriate response. The alternative was curling into a ball and indulging in self-pity, fouling bedsheets with gallons of tears. Hour after hour.

I pumped pedals at maximum velocity along Lake Superior's north shore. Feelings coursed through my veins, propelling forward motion, and visibly manifesting as tears splashing down onto pavement. Emotions ranged from elation over newfound freedom in a world of fresh possibilities, to the overwhelming dread an innocent death row inmate feels on his last walk, absorbing sights and sounds.

Everything was awash in meaning: the endless blue expanse of Lake Superior, wildflowers bending with the breeze on a gorgeous July day, a fantastically vivid green weed thriving in a crack of the road as I sped by at 20 miles per hour. A Lake-facing flower bed produced a fresh burst. The eruption of color was a massive boost. I restrained myself from stopping to hug the gardeners. Simple beauty is amazingly uplifting to someone passing by out on the edges. They'll never grasp how touching that moment was.

I returned home with a healthier perspective after churning out 22 difficult miles—body, mind, and soul, all whipped up. Renewed. I knew my career had languished within the trap of telecommuting, convenience, and security. As the sole breadwinner, taking risks seemed ridiculous. If they hadn't pushed me out, might I have become a lifer?

That night, after breaking the news to my wife, I wrote the following in a blog post dated 7/30/14:

I deeply want to be rooted vocationally in the local community working with and for people who know and care for you, rather than in solely the bottom line of a large corporation. This is what I'm exploring.

Unfortunately, I'd also like to be a farmer someday. Ha ha. My wife has no desire, but a boy can dream. In 12 years, I'd really like to buy this hobby farm that's a mere 10 miles from here…

In the years since pining over that barn and pasture, we learned to live that life right here in the city. I had only the faintest impression of how intensely difficult the journey would become.

Thank goodness.

3

An unbroken chain of work, beginning as a paperboy, had endured for a quarter-century. Each link failed to advance personal interests or any career trajectory. They were the path of least resistance.

An impressive resume was the obvious solution. Despite approaching blank page with a can-do spirit and achieving perfection in name and address fields, I stared fruitlessly at the screen for hour after painful hour.

Succinct bullet points—a blitzkrieg of braggadocio—are pheromones for attracting a disinterested hiring manager's attention. My qualities were more conducive to genial conversation over a bottle of wine, taking careful measure of pros and cons. Polishing this turd was impossible. The best-case scenario was a one-way ticket to another unfulfilling assignment, siphoning off purpose and drive for the sake of anonymous shareholders.

In jest, I came up with a line that got the ball rolling:

- ACCOMPLISHED BEDWETTER WITH 19 YEARS EXPERIENCE

"Oh, they'll like that," I thought, following it with four good'ns.

- RESTORED CHILD OF HOARDER, "WOLF BOY"
- MIRTH-MAKING ADVENTURER
- WORM WRANGLER
- HOUSE PAINTER

Contemptuously, I added:

- BICYCLE RIDER
- RAT BASTARD

Though birthed in cynicism, these were indeed qualities I might tap. A lightbulb switched on in my head. The problem became the solution. I had a story to write and a corresponding surplus of time. The sense of urgency was overwhelming. So, I stamped these onto a business card with

- AUTHOR.

The year-long process of producing my first book, <u>The Emancipation of a Buried Man</u>, felt less daunting than papering over a shipwrecked career with a single-page resume. Written with feverish intensity, it was all I had to offer the world.

While it didn't propel me into an authorial career, it pushed our new life into motion. Marketing the work was a valuable experience, requiring a shift in mindset. Of further benefit, I communicated stories from my past that had never been shared. The laborious process was remarkably cathartic.

Entrepreneurship gradually displaced the employee in me. A reliance upon others telling me what to do reached way beyond my first corporate job, into two decades of institutionalized education. My perch near the top of a large high school class showed an ability to achieve high test scores, so I replicated this success in college and graduate school. I stopped reading books for pleasure and performed for tests. In the end, this meant nothing.

It takes years to bash this out of a high-achiever.

4

Cubicle Land, ever-ravenous, digested all the tasty bits. Finally arriving at skin, bones, and gristle, the leviathan spewed me out. I washed up on the shores of a wasteland with no tangible or transferrable skills.

Tattered Red Wing boots and abused canvas painter pants waited in suspended animation. Pressing this ragged attire into service was like slipping into a superhero's suit. A painter's knowledge, confidence, and attitude came back in a flood. The Uniform made me feel competent and skilled. I had something, however humble, to offer of real value.

This dynamic duo came together back in college. Newly minted with a degree, little did I realize how valuable these skills would become over a lifetime.

The boots were castoffs, like me. Handmade in the 1960s, I'm grateful for the cow grazing beneath a scorching sun at the tail end of the Eisenhower Administration that gave everything. Its very last bits carry on, supporting my family's survival.

Heels are the life-securing feature. Up there, at altitude, you need a high heel. Leaning forward on the ladder against that thick chunk of rubber provides a secure locked-in feel.

I'm not a house painter by trade, but I reckon these boots have reaped $50,000 for our family when it mattered most. They've been laced up for every project across a quarter-century of intermittent leanness. Every drop of value has been squeezed from these works of art. The sound of the garbage truck trundling down the alley produced a pang of regret on this very day. The lace-ups awaited their lift atop a bag of excrement. I rescued them just in time, during final approach.

Reunification wrought rhapsodic joy. A photo shoot was the natural outflow. I captured their essence in an image fit for a pin-up calendar. Angling sunshine illuminates cracked leather beatifically. The boots, faithful servants to generations, are better suited for a museum than being squished into a landfill's filthy slurry.

Still overflowing with gladness and needing to get something more out of me, I sat down and began writing this book. Beginning is the hardest part. Prior to this experience, I found myself grasping at a subject too slippery. Half a notebook was filled with incoherent scribblings about money. Finally, I had something I could grab hold of. The boots helped save the day once again, nudging me back on track.

Virtually anything that produces this kind of irrational joy, a deep satisfaction with roots reaching into your soul, is worth pursuing down the rabbit hole. Learning to indulge personal eccentricities, rather than stifling them, became the key to building a lifestyle tailored to our strengths and weaknesses.

Something that might seem foolish to all onlookers could prove critical in the journey of building a life that works for you. The rest of my painting crew trashed their well-worn attire back in 1999. They didn't grow up amidst squalor like me, in a house where the only limit to obsessive hoarding was the height of our ceilings. Pathologically, I squirreled the painter whites and boots away.

The Uniform represented an entirely different skill set from the more cerebral-based life I pursued in academia. The boots enabled me to stand an inch taller, enhancing my very being, while the pants provided the means for wearing a hardscrabble work ethic on my sleeve. Breezing into the grocery store after a day of hard work was an act of a competent and confident man, garnering furtive glances from well-heeled patrons newly emerged from the office with nary a scuff on shined shoes or perfectly pleated trousers.

A year into marriage and working life, for lack of other ideas, I sought refuge in a graduate school near Boston. Upon arriving, I made one random phone call to the first painter listed in the Yellow Pages, securing a short stint. The contrast to academic life was refreshing. Once again, I enjoyed a little swagger when wearing them in public. The boots and paint-splattered pants became an emblem of capability. Deep down, I suppose I thought I was better than that, while studying within a consortium of schools that included lofty old Harvard. Someday I'd rely on my big brain exclusively. (A hated nickname as a child was, "Big Head Ed," so perhaps I mean this literally.) It felt good to use the body for the time being.

I never found my way into brainy work. Out of expediency, I filled low-level corporate jobs where a high school diploma was the only firepower necessary. Not only did I fail to use the body, my brain wasn't particularly taxed either.

Those hardscrabble painter clothes were tucked away for years, representing a hidden side of me. Pulling them out for house projects every now and again, I reveled in the sensation of cool, rugged canvas. The soft blandness of corporate casual wear was associated with boredom, cubicles, and a work life leading nowhere.

On the cusp of middle age and feeling like a castaway, I started off by painting a neighbor's garage at a low hourly rate. This led to a single side of a nearby home and other small jobs. The satisfaction of visible accomplishment—adding beauty to the real world—was uplifting. The contrast of employing my entire body to eke out some coin, as opposed to languishing before a computer, was extraordinary. Simultaneously, I reached into that oversized brain to write a book. Each effort began in the humblest manner possible. Providing value to the world while navigating this major transition (a complete teardown and rebuilding of life) was critical.

Eventually, I received work further afield than the back alley. The feeling of commuting to a job site felt entirely novel. A full day of honest labor, requiring a packed lunch, caused me to exude optimism from every pore in my body. That first bike ride home at sunset on a chilly fall day was exhilarating. With painter pants beneath me, I felt like a triumphant Napoleon atop his white horse.

The sense of pride bursting from my breast made me think of the former Emperor, who, after escaping exile from the tiny island of Elba in the Mediterranean, was met by a regiment of troops sent to intercept him. Instead, upon meeting him, they shouted, "Vive L'Empereur!" and marched with him to Paris, where he regained power for the next 100 days.

It was fantastic to re-enter the world of commerce in such a manner. The ride in both directions was brisk and invigorating as I cut through biting winds. Chugging uphill in the morning was an ideal way to break a sweat and get limbered up for a big day spent painting the interior of an apartment. Evenings found me atop my white horse in triumph, coasting much of the way back down the hill.

I was awash in satisfaction from having participated with humanity in the local economy. Throngs of people rushing home in their cars felt like brothers and sisters. I felt sorry that they were missing out on abundant fresh air, but there was kinship with them nonetheless. Twelve years of corporate work never produced this feeling of taking part alongside them. Previously, my work was for a distant Mothership, contributing to the needs of far off, amorphous shareholders who knew nothing of me or my community. Partaking in and engaging tangibly with your community, applying the fix to even the smallest problem, is a powerful contrast. It's like entering the stream with thousands of salmon, each on their own personal journey but somehow in this grand story together, navigating obstacles and perils.

While I opted to pedal out of a basic desire to save money on gas—zero expenses deducted from a day's efforts—I discovered riding bike each way provided splendid bookends to the day. It was the perfect cleaving of work and home life, enabling me to become immediately present as a worker on the one hand, and a father and husband on the other. Of further benefit, my muscles felt fine-tuned afterward, a marked contrast to the unsatisfying soreness that came from sitting in a chair all day.

Exercise became a byproduct of the greater purpose of moving from here to there. As essential as physical activity may be to physical, mental, and emotional well-being, it can be virtually impossible for the unemployed to devote significant time to the task. It feels like a personal indulgence when you should be scraping together a living for the family. It's a bit messed up, but it can be easier to justify staring at the wall or curling up in bed. The easiest way around this sad state of affairs is to couple the need to move your body with legitimate cost savings while running errands, networking, and performing odd jobs. That there is a pro-tip worthy of the cost of this book (underline, circle, and do).

When security and prospects for a ready income are taken away, small things become praiseworthy to the point of tearful joy. This is so healing for a broken heart. Wasting away in work that didn't suit me, I had become stuck within an alternative dimension that lacked connection to the real world, and was doing nothing to change my lot in life. Simple, honest, physical work became a marvelous transition in moving toward an uncertain future.

Engaging with humankind in practical and meaningful ways was a delightful contrast to my previous life. The straightforward act of regenerating a filthy room, transforming it with paint and love communicated through diligent work, gave me the feeling of blessing some future resident. I imagined them sitting down between those walls with tears streaming down at the end of a stressful day, so I prayed for them. That was my contribution. It was all I had been given to do. I performed it to the best of my ability, with purpose and love.

I never would have considered such menial work if I had dispensed with the old uniform. So, thank you Red Wing for boots that performed when called upon for over half a century, and Dickies for a $20 pair of canvas pants that enabled me to form an alter ego, and so much more.

5

Henry David Thoreau, in his quest to "Drive life into a corner," advocated an existence so simple that we could walk away empty-handed and without anxiety if the Canadians were to march down and conquer Duluth.

A classic narcissist who lacked a family to support, Thoreau had plenty of space for his arguably self-obsessed pursuits. To my great surprise, however, having a supportive wife and children became my ace in the hole. "All for one and one for all," challenges were faced as a pack.

We resolved to consider this pilgrimage a grand adventure, an opportunity to reduce life to simpler terms so we might have space to pursue our dreams. As Sigurd Olson counsels in Reflections From the North Country, "Complexity robs us of time and energy by making life so involved with the unessential, the real things are forgotten."

Chaos marked my childhood: emotional, physical, spiritual. Home was filled to the brim with the sort of dross, detritus, flotsam and jetsam that hoarders pack around themselves. Starved for companionship, I shared my bedroom with over 100 animals. I could go on. Perhaps you've read the book.

Adulthood has been a continual pruning of the unnecessary in a never-ending quest for simplicity. My job loss, combined with a reality of few tangible skills or bonafides to carry me forward, imposed the simplicity of humble circumstances.

Humility is a necessary component of the well-lived life. While meditating on ideas that promote this virtue can be beneficial, nothing beats being brought low and living it. Mother Teresa didn't become humble by reading about it. Rather than fight reality, it's liberating to embrace the wisdom that hard times can deliver.

Buying virtually nothing but food, we learned to more fully enjoy the blessings we already had. There was no hiding behind a facade of worldly success. Scripture rang with resonance.

Blessed are the poor in spirit,
For theirs is the kingdom of heaven.
Blessed are those that mourn,
For they will be comforted.
Blessed are the meek,
For they will inherit the earth.

Finding our way from a point of weakness was magical. We celebrated Christmas with consumerism tamped down to a minimum. The season grew rich in unexpected blessings that'll linger forever.

We plucked our tree from a vast boreal civilization, the Northwoods. As the kids veered off in one direction to hunt options, but found joy in sledding instead, I ducked, bowed, twisted and turned through a tangle of alder en route to a clearing where balsams might thrive under ample light.

Unabashed chickadees frittered about and heralded my arrival, as if welcoming Snow White into their secret kingdom. The morning had dawned cold, clear, and crisp. The wind was but a wisp. Sunlight swept in at a steep angle from its eight-minute journey through space and illuminated hexagonal crystals of ice and fresh snow, adorning the glade in brilliance. Worries about money and the future vanished inside an ethereal realm.

Beguiled, as if by a trance, I shuffled toward a promising option. A grouse had concealed itself beneath the gift. When it flushed—loud and sudden to the point of a cardiac episode—reality returned in a start. The portal closed as unexpectedly as it arrived. Three minutes of enchantment had been allotted. I hadn't sought it out. It found me. I merely showed up with an open heart.

While I wouldn't wish these struggles on anyone, limits and deprivation promote thanksgiving in a way that abundance cannot.

That year's trick-or-treating experience provides a perfect illustration. Food sensitivities and a general curmudgeonliness over candy on my part all conspired to deprive my daughter of most treats that other kids engorge themselves on. With a twinkle in her eye after a rigorous sifting of the bucket-filling haul, Emma hoisted two treasures into the air with an appreciative gleam in her eye. Rather than crying over 200 forbidden sweets, she exuded profound gratitude from every pore in her little body for the one percent that remained. Pure, unvarnished joy.

Moments like these—so diminutive that the worries of life might have concealed them—encouraged us not to wish our collective situation away. Spartan simplicity is nearly impossible to choose, but is easily embraced.

Rather than wish our low circumstances away, we resolved to learn from them. Every purchase was distilled down to the barest of necessities. These precious few items were paired with life choices more closely resembling our values.

I hustled for every dollar, and even banked $20 from a neighbor's simple babysitting gig. This willingness to abandon any appearance of worldly success or above average intelligence yielded surprising results.

Biking to painting jobs in full schmuck regalia—filthy painter pants festooned with splotches of paint and those tattered boots—provided quite a sight for gawkers. I traveled with a pole extending four feet in front of me like a joust, wore a backpack bursting with necessities, and pulled an overloaded trailer containing a step stool, drop cloth, ladder, and buckets. Since most gigs were in the general vicinity of my neighborhood, anonymity was impossible. My status was on full display. Most unexpectedly, this was a liberating gift.

As pretense, facade, and posturing dissolve away, a new outlook on life gradually unfurls. While I was never one to put on appearances, I lacked the courage to step out and do something radically different. Though a misfit, my life had blended into the beige and grays of normalcy. What a disaster! A willingness to wear humble circumstances on my sleeve was a key step forward.

Writing a book filled with vulnerabilities—bedwetting, hoarding, loneliness, a deep longing for meaning in life— required fearlessness. Nakedness emerged after abandoning any compulsion to blend in. Once again, hard to choose. Easy to embrace.

Half-baked ideas, previously eschewed as nonsensical, became legitimate options. Anxiety about looking like a fool while experimenting with them had evaporated. To quote Chesterton, "If a thing is worth doing, it is worth doing poorly at first." Fear of failure vanished. I already was one! A more positive aversion took its place: living among the vast multitude who die with innate talents locked away.

Action is essential. Overthinking—analysis paralysis—is death to be avoided at all costs. Just do. Iterate.

Wash.

Rinse.

Repeat.

This transitional period is awkward. Like a tadpole sprouting legs, transformation is confusing. The rush of adventurous freedom fills the vacuum left behind by certainty's absence. Aggressively paddle that boat downstream. Flow with the current instead of struggling against it. Have faith that you will not plunge over a waterfall to your death. Discover where the river takes you.

6

Losing your job with a family in tow might sound like the end of the world.

It's not.

Perhaps you envy the 22-year-old kid, minted with a college degree and walking the plank, ready to dive into a world of possibilities. Surely you'd launch off that board—somersault, twist, tuck—and with perfect awareness recover into a vertical position, melding with the water like a mermaid. No splash! The judges, in awe of beauty and grace, hoist signs bearing perfect 10's amidst rapturous applause.

Yeah, right.

It's the rare, self-possessed teenager who possesses vocational clarity amalgamated with fearless determination to pursue it in the face of scoffers, self-doubt, and the virtual omnipresence of normalcy—the veneer of which may be prosperous and carefree, but scratch beneath the surface and you'll often discover boredom, hollowness, and rot. Executing that dive with conviction is terribly difficult for those of us not meant to be, "Doctors and lawyers and such."

Life experience, and even a handful of dependents, can actually increase your odds of success. You don't have the luxury of piddling around in idealism at this stage of life. You've become more of a realist. Family and responsibilities also provide limits.

Limitless possibilities are paralyzing. Should I spend a year in Alaska, Europe, go for that exciting internship, or get a job to service student debt? The recent college grad stares into the face of infinite options, but lacks wisdom. He or she often falls into that first job, wakes up 10 or 20 years later (as if unplugged from the Matrix), and only then realizes their mistake.

As the family breadwinner with a mortgage to feed when the corporate teat went dry, I had very few options. This blessing in disguise eliminated analysis paralysis for the first time in my life. When the ratchet tightens and life becomes constrained (like when the car blew up and all our appliances seemed to fail at once, which we'll get to) the way forward becomes MORE clear. We needed immediate cash, so I applied paint to walls. There was very little hemming and hawing about life goals, spiritual gifts, and other quagmires that can bog a guy down for years. Life gets real simple when you don't have the luxury of combing through your ideals, picking out so many nits.

On the cusp of middle age, I was battle hardened. Years of frustration and disappointment stored up a battery of grit, pluck, and resolve—a vast reservoir of potential energy. Inertia, endemic in Cubicle Land, caused these riches to go unused. It was as if the train's wheels had rusted to the tracks. Hungry children have a way of jolting life back into motion. Though movement proceeded at a tortoise-pace, we kept pushing forward. Paralyzing fear was no longer a factor. The worst had already happened. We lived to tell about it.

Like the game Settlers of Catan, played without money but

with resources strategically placed on the board, we began with materials on hand. Our assets, though wee, were ample enough for that crucial first step: getting started.

We own our own home, for example. It sits upon a 50 X 140-foot lot. Could all of our economic activity emanate from this small space? In a quest for an alternative form of financial independence, we learned to generate 100% of our income from within these walls and yard. Transformation of home and property into a workhorse continues to this day.

I endured an unusually difficult childhood, followed by a magnificent extraction. This is a marvelous story. Might I make any hay out of that? There's no way of knowing without trying. While I crafted my first book at the extreme rear of our property, atop the garage overlooking the back alley, Shawna created increasingly marketable artwork at the opposing pole of our estate.

If there's one thing I've done right, and this is more a symptom of us being made for each other than any virtue, it's that I encouraged her to be an artist long before it made financial sense.

She put the paintbrush down for the first six years of our marriage to work secretarial jobs. Shawna only resumed her true calling after having twins made these low-paying jobs impossible to perform. She stayed home with the kids while I hacked a path through a tangled mess of a career without a compass, bringing home $35 - $40K a year. Around the time when the children could have gone to preschool, she began painting more regularly. Her subjects were simple observations: a stuffed bunny discovered in amusing locations, a fort made from a chair and blanket, the canary belting out tunes a few feet from her desk, an antique chair in the morning sun.

Mothers are often at a crossroads as their children approach school age. Shawna faced similar perplexities. Her giftedness made the calculation pretty straightforward. Returning to work meant trading her time for a low wage. Instead of reducing someone else's stress in service as a secretary, thus transferring anxiety to the family whenever a kid was sick or school was closed, the obvious choice was for her to remain at home. Her skill set, far more valuable than ten to twelve dollars an hour, rendered her unemployable. The equation was elegant for its simplicity. There was very little to contemplate. Challenging decisions often contain their own solutions. Wait patiently, and they'll rise to the surface.

While I rested confidently, this became a personal struggle for Shawna. I beamed with pride while praising her talent in public, but she consistently faced doubt-reinforcing reactions. Some were subtle. Others, not so much. Intelligent women with something to contribute had careers with benefits. She battled an inferiority complex whenever forced to explain that her time went into raising twin children and creating art. This became increasingly difficult to articulate after the kids went off to school.

Several years in, annual sales amassed as hundreds of dollars. Pressing on, she attained limited notoriety, but plateaued at $1000 for ages. The kids progressed into middle school.

A topic of conversation became her style, rather unique among Northwoods painters who often succeed by selling landscapes. Galleries expressed appreciation, but demurred.

At a critical moment of doubt, I enjoined, "Imagine a world where your business grew tenfold to a whopping $10,000. That would be awesome, but would it change our lives?"

"No."

"Just have fun with it. Play with your paintings. Produce works that bring you joy. The income will take care of itself, eventually. Your best work happens when you are whimsical and unconcerned with sales."

This is solid advice for anyone in the early stages of a creative career. A decade spent honing her craft in obscurity was required for making the giant leap forward when we needed it.

Trusting the audience would come, I pushed her to make quirky paintings reflecting one-of-a-kind observations of things that moved her. I wasn't the World's Greatest Husband, or particularly prescient. Her talent was obvious.

While watching the show Alias, Shawna once remarked, "I could never be a spy." It has been a running joke for 20 years. The declarative statement applies to virtually any career. Her uniqueness renders her unsuited for traditional work, which we regard as unbearably boring. These qualities attracted me to her. Why would I consider squelching creativity for a newer car? That way of thinking, though palliative to short-term stress, is short-sighted.

Future success depended on Shawna devoting 30 - 40 hours each week to perfecting her craft. Ten years of playfully pushing paint around on wood panels earned no significant income beyond the cost of supplies. She persevered. Faithfully, and with conviction.

My wife's early works were quite good, but failed to command decent prices. She still hadn't found her voice. Friends and family comprised the audience.

I didn't begrudge Shawna for tallying up thousands of hours, creating artwork for virtually no return. The kids and I immensely enjoy her paintings, many of which are fantastically weird and amazing. Frankly, it was easy to be supportive of her work.

I'm looking at a favorite photo of my young daughter. She's ferociously engrossed in a book. Three of Shawna's paintings rest in the background. These are other-worldly imaginative pieces, now on permanent display in the Hall of Rejects. The most visible painting contains two alien children with large oblong heads. One holds a hand over the other's eyes, which you can see right through the hands. Bubbles run up the arm into roots that penetrate the sibling's brain. The painting conveys a mysterious communication developed between our twins. What a privilege to have first witnessed the reality, and now to possess an image that captures the essence.

Shawna's work enmeshes with family life like a gear to a

cog. Often inspiring and breathing it in, our kids have grown up adjacent to the successes and failures of her entire body of work.

Not that it was all roses and unicorns. Amidst constant interruptions, balls careening as paint dried, and kids running out their energy, she worked at a small table in our dining room. Chaos! Still, I envied how her contribution to the world connected with the family. My work was invisible, confined to computers, and cordoned off by cubicles. Disconnected. Unexplainable.

Then, in the blink of an eye, that corporate gravy train came to a screeching halt. It was so heartless, and... INCONVENIENT. We were days from commencing a $6,000 home renovation designed to provide Shawna with an art studio. This was a serious multiple of her annual sales that consumed most of our savings. We had already plunked down half the money, so there was no choice but to proceed. A month earlier, we would have cancelled this optional project, causing Shawna to languish in obscurity for years to come. If the layoff came later, we'd have been robbed of the rich experience of stepping out in faith. This wasn't owing to any virtue or wisdom. Options were exhausted. Needle threaded ever so carefully, the Engineer behind this calamity dwarfs the corporation that carried it out.

Our entire pursuit of a sustainable household economy is inconceivable without this studio. What now seems like a modest step of common sense was then the whole ball of wax. Walking down this road, one to which we were pushed, connected our faith to the real world. There was no other choice but moving forward by working to the best of our abilities, and trusting that things would work out. Never alone. Together.

This investment lit a fire beneath Shawna that has never gone out. In order to justify the expense, she doubled down on her discipline while cranking out more paintings than ever before. The uptick in quantity resulted in uncommon quality. Dozens of works came out of the new studio, several exhibitions went onto the calendar, and breaks came her way.

Her discipline—hours at the easel—is unmatched. While I struggled with a sidelining depression, she'd put eight hours of work in after sending the kids off to school with lunches, and whipped up full, stunning, nutritious meals in the evenings. Shawna Gilmore is great at her work because she puts in the time. Daily. This has never been a hobby for her. I'm not as good a writer as she is an artist because I am not nearly as disciplined.

After putting in a decade of quiet, unsung work, Shawna 10X'd her sales over the course of the next year. She was ready to produce at the moment we needed her. Seemingly overnight, she transformed from unknown artist on the fringes into a well-known creator and contributor to our community's rich conversation over art, and now meets half our family's needs. Lightning hadn't struck, nor was she "picked" by the gatekeepers. My wife had been perfecting her craft for years. She was bursting with talent and ability. Our family's lack of income merely opened the door to her potential. The snowball continues to grow, slowly and sustainably, at a pace she can manage.

No big moment of fame has catapulted either of us. Simple forward progress, inch by painstaking inch, is building a bonafide household economy.

It has been a long slog, but my work is finally being spun within the family's direct orbit. I write these lines in our dining room. Early morning is my special time. Everybody trundles down the stairs at their own leisure, well after sunrise, finding me finishing up for the day. I discuss the rawness of my craft with them, what I accomplished, and how I'll never improve without consistent effort. Though success is far from a surety, I work this out with fear and trembling every day. This is marvelous.

Would I possess enough fortitude to pursue this kind of work on my own? I think not. The blank screen is daunting. Tens of thousands of small decisions, the grist of a book, are debilitating. Without wife and daughter demanding their share of the pot, a never-ending stream of coffee would destroy my digestive tract. Moderation is a healthy imposition. More significantly, I can't afford as much beer as I'd like to consume. Robbing my children of funds more profitably invested elsewhere is off the table. I've stared at this screen, paced the house, and beat my head against the wall while wrestling with this complex chapter for weeks. Liquor's siren call, a false promise of lubrication, hangs in the air. Writers are a magnet to addiction. The perilous shortcut isn't a viable option to the family man. Thank goodness.

The gateway to Tiny Farm Duluth is a dozen feet from where I struggle to assemble these words. French doors open into a newly completed sunroom that contains my day job: Tiny Farm Duluth. After writing, breakfast, and some coffee talk, I retreat to this year-round agricultural enterprise. Years of struggle went into compressing a profitable farm into this space. Chrome shelves run floor to ceiling and across the entire 17-foot south-facing span. A wall of glass pulls in every available drop of sunshine. 168 linear feet of light-emitting diodes illuminate green, purple, and ruby red microgreens. Occasionally, the sun goes down before I have a chance to pull the shades, creating a fishbowl effect. The glow is viewable from outer space.

The turntable feels like the heartbeat of the operation. I move and groove while accomplishing tedious work, a dance with brain and body in tandem. That's the ideal, anyway. I'm pleased my kids can easily observe what I do, imperfect and humble as it may be.

On the other side of this wordsmithing assembly line, 15 feet away in near-perfect symmetry, rests another pair of French doors. These swing into the art studio carved out of our front porch. The most profitable investment of our lives, Shawna makes use of every square inch. Just as I never could have launched a farm in the city on my own (and then have the insight to shrink it down Lilliputian-like), Shawna was incapable of reaching her full potential by herself. We would fail without one another's daily love and support. By ourselves, we'd epitomize the very definition of starving artists. Together, however, we're thriving even as the battle goes on.

The notion of either of us earning a full income by ourselves, even a small one, feels impossible. But can each of us earn half an income? Yes! Indeed, we can. Even that diminished target is only achievable as we support one another every day, bearing with the other's frailties and weaknesses. Those glaring faults in the other are often strengths in ourselves. We've transformed into two horses hitched to the team, pulling a single load as one.

While this requires lifestyle sacrifice and avoiding comparison like the plague, the benefits to our marriage are legion. We have satisfaction in exercising our God-given gifts through continual struggle together. There's a deep pool of skill and passion still waiting to be tapped. Slowly, inch by inch, we sink our wells deeper into what once seemed impenetrable.

7

Farming captivated me long before I could effectively navigate a pitchfork loaded with silage. As I struggled down the concrete pier into a sea of ravenous cows, wide-set bovine eyes followed this tiny being's every movement. After setting the steaming goodness before them, wildly disproportionate to the needs of 40,000 pounds of beef on the hoof jostling one another, the beasts grew restless. My rate of replacement failed to keep pace with consumption. Mournful moos, snorting, and crazed eyes bespoke impatience. I was like a hapless comedian who lost the audience.

Finally, Grandpa arrived with his huge load of corn. He finished the job with boundless strength. His way of doing things hadn't changed in a hundred years. Timelessness, redolent with the earthy smells of fermenting silage mingled with dung, permeated the atmosphere. The bustling metropolis on all sides was ever-changing, greedy to bite off another chunk of the homestead. Grandpa lived across the street. It was easier for him to drive the short distance to the farm, where his mother still lived, rather than attempt crossing both lanes of busy Milwaukee Street on foot.

My great-great-great grandfather, a Civil War veteran, purchased the land under the Homestead Act. The last major holdout in the metro area, Wisconsin's capitol building is just three miles away. 65 surviving acres are only now in the planning stages of development. This place provided a sense of peace and stability amidst constant change for 150 years.

Just as this farm was a bulwark in a harried ocean of modernity, visits to my other grandparents up north were an oasis from chaos. We enjoyed long hours in the largest and most beautiful vegetable garden I've ever seen. A handful of extended stays, involving simple work in the soil away from television, may have been the finest moments of my childhood. They were a reprieve from loneliness and lack of purpose. The simplicity of their daily rhythms made me into a man of the soil. Tragically, the rest of life was notable for its acute absence.

In a misguided attempt at cultivating this sense of peace, I accumulated 100 animals in my bedroom. If only I had started a vegetable garden instead! Shame kept me cloistered behind closed doors, hidden away from neighbors. No guiding hand encouraged exploration of interests.

College brought liberation from mountains of stuff. It was a grand beginning, but a craving to be out on the land grew ravenous. Wilderness exploration became my focus. Classes and school work faded into the background. Like scratching an itch, this need became so overwhelming that the civilization of higher education was abandoned for a time. The vast wilderness of border country beckoned. I hunkered into a cabin with books and frenetically travelled through the forest. Perhaps I was beating back a raging case of ADHD. Farming was all but forgotten. Little did I know, it sat dormant inside me, with the patience of a virus.

Grad school brought an opportunity to manage the landlord's flower gardens and lawn. No matter how busy I became with studies, there was always time to nourish the soil and minister to the needs of my "congregants." Working the land outside in the elements with my wife became a favorite pastime. One solitary and silent hour, however, stands out in highlight.

Prostrate beneath a large bush, my body soaked up the ground's warmth, delighting in full contact. As a penetrating sun heated my backside, I found myself face to face with a common toad exercising dominion over a tiny kingdom.

Never have I witnessed such focus and concentration. It sat perfectly still upon its throne, awaiting the movement of nourishment. Once detected, the large toad's eyes fixed on its prey. The impassive face screwed into an expression akin to someone experiencing a bowel movement, fully devoted to the task in both thought and deed. Avoiding the urge to blink, I remained frozen as the amphibian unfurled its incredible tongue to bring in the tasty morsel.

All worries about money and schoolwork evaporated into some other world. I laid there motionless and silent for at least an hour, though there was much to do at semester's end. Spellbound, I lingered as the toad devoured another dozen insects. Other than a slight cock of the head, fixing of the eyes, and a lightning-fast tongue, my friend barely budged. Sustenance came to the toad, for which he waited patiently.

Marveling at the splendid simplicity of this being, life slowed down. Peace returned. Rich in beauty as any mountaintop I've stood upon, the creator's handiwork was on full display. The spiritual experience, ethereal yet rooted in the solid terra firma of earth, rivals anything I've encountered. I was face down in the dirt, two feet from a fellow creature fulfilling its purpose. In the soil together, we were both of the creation, placed within peculiar kingdoms by our common maker.

I felt hidden away in some magical world, even though

90% of my body extended from beneath the rhododendron in full view of passersby. A portal between worlds had opened. Meanwhile, people just walked on by. Oblivious.

These moments of an altered state of being, when time stops as you become enthralled in an activity or spectacle that others ignore, are milestones. Ignore them at your peril! Regardless of how crazy such interests may seem, there's something inherent that will help unlock your hidden potential or gift to the world.

8

Grandma died as I finished my book.

Baked into immersion within a larger-than-life project—writing a book, feeding a family in an emergency, or renovating a house perhaps—is inevitable collision with stark reality. The wheel of time remains in motion. Life outside your myopic view isn't static. Attention focuses like a laser beam on the work and staying afloat. Finally, you look up and discover that the rest of the world isn't waiting in suspended animation. Progress marches on relentlessly.

Her life spanned a century. 1915 - 2015. Spanish Influenza ravaged the population. World War I raged. A revolution rocked Russia. Automobiles were rare, possessed by a wealthy few. Most families in her neck of the woods didn't have a telephone. Another lifetime like hers brings you to Thomas Jefferson.

Born 67 years after Wisconsin became a state, Grandma Eunice grew up among the Big Woods of Laura Ingalls Wilder. Crandon, seat of Forest County, was not far removed from those frontier days. Corduroy roads were still in use. Her Grandfather boasted of shaking Abraham Lincoln's hand after the Battle of Gettysburg.

She was a twin, like my kids, and announced this commonality with them about every five minutes. "Oh, they're twins? I was a twin. They get that from me!" Her brother, my namesake, was killed in action during World War II.

Grandma was always there for us. Even after her mind changed with old age, it was a comfort knowing she was still alive and kicking.

She married a carpenter named Alloys after her first husband passed away. From the time of their wedding just prior to my birth, until about the year 2000, they barely seemed to change. My grandparents were kind, wise, and steady. They were like bedrock, the most stable force in my life.

An inexhaustible supply of healthy food graced their table, as if carried in by the King's servants. Tablecloth laid out, large serving bowls of potatoes, broccoli, peas, gravy, and a scrumptious roast or stew consumed every square inch. I ate like a prince.

Grandma labored in that kitchen on Metonga Avenue for seven decades. She was always there, white-haired and all, fulfilling her role as grandmother.

I cherished a glorious week with them every summer until it was torn away, a casualty of squabbling divorced parents. Cousins bemoaned lengthy stays with Grandma and Grandpa. Indeed, they had nothing going on. Time pivoted around the garden, fount of all that fresh produce on their table. I spent most of each day with them in that wellspring of abundance. They possessed a mysterious wizardry, enabling them to coax and charm a stunning variety of fruits and vegetables from the soil. It was a labor of love.

Though the quantity of visits dwindled, quality was outstanding. She was among precious few tethers in life, anchoring me in love and a more solid reality.

The dinner experience is a prized memory, informing the ideal. Healthily and lovingly prepared food mingled with relaxed table talk. There were no distractions other than, on rare occasions, a knock at the screen door. Seated with coffee or pie, they merged into the quorum. Today we call it the Slow Food Movement, but this was everyday life for my grandparents. We lingered for an hour after the meal was over, sipping tea. Nobody had to be anywhere. This was the place for being. Conversation continued over a lengthy game of Rummikub or cards.

As Grandma made sure everyone was comfortable and well-fed, Grandpa shared war stories. He served in North Africa during World War II and pushed up the boot of Italy among Patton's forces. A devout Catholic, he was among a handful selected to meet the Pope. His stories were enthralling.

At 25, my last visit before Grandpa Alloys died, I recorded a tape of dynamic after-dinner conversation. It is among my most cherished possessions. The morning after, amidst comfortable silence punctuated by insects plying invisible highways, I sat beside him on the porch. Tears welled up uncontrollably, spilling over the dam. It was our last moment together. I was bound for graduate school on the East Coast. Cancer ravaged his body. With unabashed tenderness, he gazed straight into me with unguarded love, passing the torch, searing the image into my mind. I staved off weeping, but tears flow whenever it comes to mind, even now, complicating the repeated reviewal of these lines. He knew it was our last good sit together. It was such an affectionate stare into my soul, and not a single word was spoken.

Oh, how I loved him.

That moment is emblematic of our relationship. We talked, but nonsensical prattling on was blissfully absent. Music surfaced in spaces between the notes. I don't recall many wise words. It was their steady presence—unconditional love—that held me transfixed.

If only I could amass enough treasure to trade for ten more visits on that back porch, undespoiled by cluttering chatter. It was box seating for overlooking the garden, a visual feast at the center of an operatic performance by pollinators, songbirds, cumulonimbus clouds in motion, and more. I will never again have a grandparent. They're all gone.

The next generation rises beneath our shade, receptive of calm guidance, with or without words.

The morning of Grandma's funeral found me alone in her kitchen, washing dishes. That old tape recorded fourteen years earlier played in the background. In no rush to hurry off to the formal event, I lingered at that sink as long as possible, saying goodbye in my own way.

Familiar conversational notes within that never-changing kitchen cascaded into mind and soul. The recording's impetus had been foreknowledge of Grandpa's likely passing. In retrospect, it was capturing them together and replaying it at this singular moment in time that is so impactful.

One or two salty tears, bubbling up from a wellspring, splashed into the water as I completed this basic necessity. This is what Grandma specialized in. As the conversation played on, with everyone pouring out their hearts in concert specifically for this weighty moment, I heard the clinking sounds of Grandma washing dishes while we relaxed at the table with tea and cookies. She added occasional remarks to the gregarious chatter from her post at the sink, but her role was more supportive than starring.

Time stopped. I was transported. Grandma and I stood at the same sink on the same worn out patch of linoleum. Our hands, along with identical utensils and other implements, descended into the depths of soapy water, from which they were drawn out. Renewed.

Both experiences are as vivid in my mind as when they transpired.

I entered the chore out of obligation with a sense of loss. By the time I finished, still lingering but desperately needing to wrangle the family for the final sendoff, I had gained much. I didn't lose my grandmother. She is still with me. Between me and her are two generations begat and begotten from her DNA. Memories and feelings live on forever.

The defining deficit of our relationship was physical: hundreds of separating miles. This loss of regular contact, a tragedy, draws me to the power of place, and sinking down deep roots. Modernity's mobility has robbed us of much identity.

My love for Grandma has nothing to do with anything she ever said or did. She was just always present and available. Embedding ourselves into a community for the long haul can be like this. People care for and support one another in a way impossible to accomplish over email, text, or Zoom.

9

Never have I been more excited to receive packages. I tore into that first shipment of books immediately, stuffed ten paperbacks into my backpack, and set off by bicycle to put them into the hands of readers. Considering that each transaction resulted in a few dollars of profit, seven hours spent crisscrossing the city might sound like a poor use of time. Perhaps it was, but time was abundant. Relationships were few.

Writing is a solitary business that drives me right to the edge of Lake Insanity. Cabin fever burned red hot by the time finished product arrived. Spring had sprung. I was like a cow released from the barn to that first flush of tender grass. Utterly exhausting, but thoroughly uplifting. Just what the doctor ordered.

These deliveries provided unexpected visiting opportunities. The one-on-one conversations were more engaging and satisfying than I ever imagined. Near strangers opened doors into their lives after sensing sincere effort. The personal touch compelled many to dive into the book that very day. Feedback the next morning was overwhelming. Several wrote to say they stayed up all night, or found themselves useless in accomplishing anything but plowing through the story. The shot of encouragement more than made up for the ridiculous expenditure of time and energy.

Virtually no rhyme or reason went into my delivery route. In one example of carelessness, I rushed a book out to a customer leaving on vacation. An hour later, I backtracked several miles to Matt, her neighbor. How stupid!

Inefficiency reaped unexpected rewards. Happy accidents like this guided me toward relinquishing control over events in order to capture the magic of serendipity. I caught Matt at just the right time, while he cooked down maple syrup from hundreds of gallons of sap. He was even more starved for conversation than I was. An earlier arrival would have been inconvenient for him. Discovery of a kindred spirit may have otherwise eluded me.

Normally a well-dressed guy with a fancypants corporate job, it was alarming to catch him looking so extravagantly hillbilly in overalls, closer to his true self. When we got to the financial transaction, he was a dollar short. At my suggestion, we enjoyed a beer together in lieu of GW's portrait. The resulting conversation that followed produced a friendship, many visits, and a partnership as chicken farmers. Who knows? Perhaps the future was altered that day. He sent me on my way with a quart of homemade sauerkraut, which we treasured for weeks. I'm pretty sure I came out ahead on the deal, but Matt enjoyed the read.

Another striking feature of this initial foray into distribution by bike was the sheer diversity of customers. The ninth stop of the day was at the Amundsen's, owners of Locally Laid Egg Company. They invited me in for a tall glass of Duluth Municipal water—some of the best on Earth—and handed me an orange the size of a grapefruit. I tore into its sweet, juicy flesh like a prisoner of war. The real treat, however, was basking in simple companionship with a couple whom I had grown to admire from afar.

Before leaving, while eyeing the sun setting alarmingly low on the horizon, I caught the irony of Jason bringing home a rotisserie chicken for a late supper after slogging through yet another day in knee-high rubber boots in service to thousands of laying hens. Fifteen minutes later, I was in the well-heeled home of a hotel executive who works in a tailored suit and shined shoes, but whose family was no less fascinating.

Active participation in the local economy—both producing and consuming—is remarkably effective at establishing rootedness. More important than fifty bucks in profit were the relationships nurtured by these simple, earnest visits. This was a surprising benefit to my delivery approach. Decisions between slower options and efficiency became clear. Efficiency comes with almost no fringe benefits.

My return to headquarters, after careening down Duluth's steep hillside at breakneck speed, coincided with the exact moment daylight was extinguished. Physical exhaustion was similarly complete. Excess energy burned off, I was free to enjoy the next moment of serendipity, rather than become annoyed.

Mom had called on December 20th. "The kids' Christmas presents are going to be a little late this year." Nothing out of the ordinary there. Grandma has a bit of an "organizational" problem. We roll with it.

Irony of ironies, the first 100 copies of my book about being a child of a hoarder finding purpose, etc, arrived alongside three boxes from my mother four months later. After all that effort and waiting, the odds of these boxes materializing together in a 4-foot stack upon our porch on the same day in April are staggering. Perhaps this points to our Maker's sense of humor.

These annual boxes carry the sensation of the hoard arriving: quantity over quality, an unmistakable aroma, randomness stuffed to the brim by a connoisseur of the Dollar Store with no labels denoting intended recipient, plastic trinkets not worth the cost of shipping. Observing the great unpacking after physically going after an alternative existence, rejecting over-abundance in my very core, was surreal. As if to provide an object lesson to reinforce our family's pursuit, the entire living room came to resemble the great stockpile I walked away from two decades earlier. Trifles, toys, and packaging changed the very character of our home.

But, she's trying to maintain a connection. We appreciate the effort.

10

Traversing the world on two wheels affords time for the mind to wander, bringing heightened awareness. Beauty penetrates armor. With one's head uncoupled from complex trivialities of daily life, these gentle arrows pass straight to the heart. The brain's filter, with its predilection for practicality and tyrannies of the urgent, is bypassed. Perception intensifies and expands, as the pragmatic chunk of the brain that keeps us alive is preoccupied with locomotion and navigational safety. Brain and body settle into a pleasing rhythm, finally agreeing to set their disputes aside, and work together.

While pedaling to the Mayor's office, I noticed a father and toddler enjoying a tender moment beside Lake Superior. The scene was so heartwarming that it pulled me out of commuter-mode, welling into delight of the journey itself. This is the sweet spot. Bearing witness to unexpected moments of grace, beauty, goodness, and kindness, fills us with gratitude. Taking in the slightest glimpse can accomplish this.

With observational skills brought to the fore, and emotions cresting atop a wave hurtling me onward, I came across an oft-sighted fellow in business attire walking the Lakewalk. I zipped by him rather frequently and finally found the nerve to stop and chat him up. I discovered he was a busy engineer with a demanding schedule who carved out the time to walk four miles to the office each way, and sometimes kayaked or biked.

Moving on to his concept of minimalism, he pointed at his heart. "The goal is to live big in here." Though his job paid well, two or three changes of clothes comprised his wardrobe. He lived about as lightly in the western world as a man can. His countenance shined with contentment. More stuff would only clutter his life, prove distracting, and thus diminish happiness.

Minutes later, bounding City Hall's steps two at a time, I was still thrilling in the unexpected conversation. "God, this is what I want to do with my life!" burst from my chest. I hadn't even arrived at the main course, 15 minutes with the Mayor, but my heart was full.

Unless you live in a mega-city, you might arrange a similar meeting. Their demanding job, besides flashy events and CEO responsibilities, includes visiting with community members whose lives have broken down by the side of the road. It keeps them humble and close to everyday people.

Mayor Don Ness was visibly skeptical of my three-legged stool: writing, house painting, and Shawna's artwork. Behind his eyes, I saw he briefly considered counseling me in another direction. Sensing naive optimism, Ness perceived I wasn't ready for that.

Eight years later, there is still no way of knowing whether his inclination was correct, or if my ongoing naïveté is the way forward. It is best to fail fast and move on. Am I merely failing slowly? I suppose it depends on one's metrics. There is no right answer. As Yvon Chouinard says, "True adventure begins when everything goes wrong." Not all adventures conclude in rapturous joy, that's for sure. That said, this arduous journey continues as a source of immense fulfillment. We soldier on.

Meeting Don in person changed me. The impetus was a bald attempt at placing my book into the hands of an influential person. While I walked away with a snazzy photo of him holding a copy before the City's Seal, the attempt at guerrilla marketing did little to boost sales. Fortuitously, the visit solidified a connection with both him and the office, as I came to understand the meaning of "public servant" for the very first time.

This sort of visit is especially valuable if you didn't vote for your mayor. Acquaint yourself with the individual on a human level while coming to understand their motivations, passions, and fears. Their competence and love for your community might surprise you. Being Mayor is remarkably challenging. Most aren't serving for the sake of personal advancement.

11

Nonstop rain, propelled sideways by 40-mile-per-hour gusts screaming off the Lake, drilled into the earth relentlessly. I paced the house for hours. 33 degrees and raw. Finally, I suited up. Trepidation prior to this delivery, the 20th, was the first chink in my armor of naïveté.

What was I doing?

Why?

No "answers" materialized. I hopped on the bike and willed myself forward. The ordeal became a metaphor for enduring a midlife crisis in real time, a gentle reminder that leading a family down the road less travelled isn't so insane after all.

Pedaling along the North Shore, straight into the tempest, the ride became immensely enjoyable. Instead of fighting the wind, I accepted it as a limiting factor. Barely exceeding the speed of a pedestrian, a motivated mall-walker perhaps, I bumbled along in the easiest gear as 13-foot waves consummated a voyage across the world's largest inland sea.

Escape velocity, punching through the city's outer rings of orbit, required energy. This, along with exposure to the elements, tore down barriers. Only lacking a shoebox, Robin welcomed me into her home with the hospitality reserved for a wounded bird. The telecommuter planned to exhaust her 15-minute break on the exchange, but we went way beyond, developing an unexpected friendship.

Connecting with someone still inside that world from which I had been cut off, guillotine-like, remains meaningful to this day. That feeling of disembowelment, crippling to forward motion, doesn't disappear on its own.

Heart, mind, and soul experienced real healing. I could have wept. Having someone in the corporate world take an interest in my story was more of a boost than I ever imagined. My stubborn refusal to squander any profit on gasoline produced dividends yet again.

This pain-staking method of delivering books helped me connect with supporters whom I never knew existed. Time on the bike also granted space to think, provided stress-relief through exercise, and fostered connection with the real world.

After being warmed by the fire of conversation, refreshed by the well of friendship, I turned down the steep gravel road leading back to Lake Superior. A truck, "Welders on Wheels," thundered by, triggering longings for usefulness. That kind of work is practical! Productive. I imagined chatting with the man over coffee, but he had places to be. Small encounters like these leave an impact on a guy poised to bring home a few dollars from an entire morning's effort. My accomplishment wasn't equivalent to killing a lion and dragging it home, but you've got to start somewhere.

The Postal Service truck, witnessed daily, similarly caused my heart to beam in admiration. Even today, the man's purposeful walk from house to house—touching lives at every stop—makes me happy.

I admire the man in the pickup truck who stopped to assist the woman stranded with three kids along a busy road. With a toolbox at his side and Leatherman on his belt, he exuded competence and calm. Breath escaped as steam from beneath the opened hood. Ten seconds of observation were more than enough to sense her gratitude.

Circling back, my cheapness over operating a 3,000-pound car felt like actual stupidity. Weakness was strength. When striking out on one's own, independent of orders, your way of doing things might seem crazy. Try not to explain or justify these quirks. They stamp the work with authentic humanity. Idiosyncrasies don't hold up against cost/benefit analysis, but are critical to formation. Where will your particular insanity carry you?

12

Wage-earners erect a wall of separation between work and family life with every shift. "Mr. Gorbachev, tear down this wall!"

Seamless integration brings a more visceral sense of gains and losses. And while setbacks often seem to overwhelm the victories, these become precious over the grand sweep of time.

A clanking sound resounded from the basement two hours before my book-launching party. Meanwhile, our 9-year-olds were gathering a large retinue of friends to greet the baby chicks. Life-upending wheels were in motion.

The unfamiliar reverberation was our dog's head glancing off the gong-like heat lamp. As soothing classical music played for the benefit of two-day-old yellow fluffballs, the canine dove in. Shawna reached the horrific scene first, gutting her. Evisceration isn't pretty.

At the moment of my wife's emergence from the basement, crying uncontrollably, kids burst through the front door in jubilation. Picture the Super Bowl's gates opening for that first wave of fanatics. The sudden appearance of a weeping mother turned the situation on its head. So many tears! Without thinking, I loaded our sullen clan into the car to find replacements: Band-Aids for broken hearts. We also picked up a pair of ducklings at the feed store, heaping on another layer of stress, but those mallards transformed despair into excitement.

What a distraction! A temporary separation of clucks from ducks required duplicating my efforts. Chicks went to the henhouse, and I located extra waterers, feeders, and heat lamps. After settling everyone, I had a half-hour to shower, eat, and ready myself for the book-launching party. I hadn't planned a thing. What readings should I choose?

Incredibly, it was a smashing success anyway. I only had to show up. A fantastic band entertained the hundred and one in attendance, carrying most of the water. My favorite coffee shop, Amity Coffee, took care of everything else. There was no time to stress over details. Venue packed to capacity and bike rack full, people spilled onto the sidewalk on a gorgeous spring day. Everyone was immensely supportive. I could simply enjoy the festivities and celebrate a milestone. It was informal and messy, like me.

Impressive events aren't as make-or-break as one might think. I sold ten books at the "launching." Most attendees who wanted a copy had already purchased one. Shawna and I continually learn this lesson. We've never experienced a big, crucial break, lives catapulted by some massive moment of publicity. It's more important to keep pressing on, perfectly illustrated only a few days later.

I secured a TV spot on a morning show. My moment had arrived! Under the impression they wanted my bike and snazzy trailer in the studio, I biked to the station before dawn in an intense Nor'easter. 40 mile-per-hour winds nearly blew me over as I travelled high and exposed along Skyline Parkway. Pelting rain, sideswiping winds, 36 miserly degrees, and a final exhausting climb up Observation Road laid me waste. Nervous bowels requiring evacuation at 5:00 AND 5:15 am, coupled with a bridge that was out, conspired to make me 10 minutes late, an eternity in TV land. They crossed me off the list. After some desperate pleading, I was slotted in again, but only if I could ready myself in two minutes.

Moments after the weather gal closed her segment with perspiration instead of precipitation, I sat in the frame (a wet and embarrassing mess) beside the clean and attractive host. The opening question about bedwetting reduced me to stammering. I had never spoken of it, and here I was on live television!

Profound emotional and physical effort went into the three-minute spot, from which I believe two additional books sold. The moral of the story, kids, is to focus on doing the work. Don't plan on being plucked from the masses, held forth by gatekeepers as a bright light, royalty checks piling high. My children witnessed this live on television before school. Later, watching the replay, we laughed at my ineptitude for the medium.

There is no single shot at success. We place our best foot forward every day. Even when our efforts are inadequate or downright disappointing, we continue advancing.

13

Mediocrity is an irresistible black hole at the center of a life spent carrying out orders.

The antidote to a lifetime's imperceptible slouch toward Failure (unique gifts untapped and buried forever) is learning to fail gracefully. Straight-A students like me might execute a series of directions to perfection, but this doesn't necessarily translate into crafting an adventurously fulfilling life. It handcuffs creativity. Extricating myself from this disposition, sticky with the decades, is no cakewalk.

Inoculation to fear of failure begins through micro-doses. Fallout from minor setbacks is virtually nonexistent, but skill and resilience find fertile ground.

We would do well to endure hundreds of small failures. We're not high atop trapeze without a net. It's more like slack-lining two feet above the ground. Falling off isn't an existential crisis.

After that first wave of hoopla and attaboys from friends, family, and acquaintances died down, for example, I carried my book into the wider world.

Arriving at the coffee shop, I optimistically laid claim to the only table available, set conveniently beside the door. Three minutes in, already fixating on the time, hope vanished. Throughout a 90-minute book-signing, I failed to deface a single copy with an autograph. Not only was the event not advertised, the gracious barista didn't even know I was coming. 9:43, 9:52, 10:06, 10:16… The wheel of time ground to a halt. My only desire was connection. The stack of books and display created a barrier. To passersby, I was a salesman. Best to avoid.

It didn't take long to understand why carnival hucksters become so aggressive at attracting attention.

Desperate to spend money on souvenirs, tourists sifted through a modest display of Duluth-themed Tchotchkes. Every one of them—a hundred left empty-handed, cash burning holes in pockets—avoided eye contact with the authentic Duluth author.

With three minutes to go, a beautiful family seated themselves a few feet away. The mother was drawn to the book's cover, an image painted by my wife. On the cusp of asking if she wanted to give it a look-see, she began nursing her baby. How could I approach her now? After Mom switched from right to left, I regained my pluck and set a copy beside her, and lingered twenty minutes beyond my thank-God-it's-over time slot.

"We'll think about it."

Grateful for the opportunity to speak with a human, I snapped a photo with their phone and had them email it to me.

This simple failure cost me nothing. It was a valuable opportunity to sit through a worst-case scenario. Was this a disaster? Boring, yes. Calamitous? No.

The acquisition of wisdom informed my reaction to Mayor Ness's upcoming suggestion that we do a book event together. Two years later, my approach toward manning a farmers market booth also had a head start. Failure paves the road to success. Unless you're testing parachutes, these disappointments are far from derailing. They prepare us for taking on more challenging and fulfilling tasks later.

14

A sunny afternoon emerged from a week of clouds and rain as I rode home from the failed book-signing. Like coming across a lemon drop in a barren cupboard, such favorable conditions were rarely squandered. As chief launderer, I looked forward to these days with expectancy. Hanging laundry is cathartic, an exquisite opportunity for putting sunlight to use.

Two months after clicking, "Publish," book sales were drying up. The goal of a year's income for a year's devotion was a pipe dream. Writing would not sustain our survival. Two hours of fruitless book-hawking was a cold dose of reality. This increasing realization was critical for charting a way forward, but crushing. I couldn't exactly fall back on my history degree.

Life transformation is demanding work. The sort of labor typically associated with vocational transition—resume writing, job fairs, attaining a certain look—was of no use to me. My issues ran deeper than selecting the pig's lipstick or placing resume into the right hands. Possibilities existed beyond my limited imagination, far-removed from a job history that had veered from the path.

Pinning individual socks to a clothesline might seem like a waste of energy at this perplexing moment. After years of pondering my plight, I understood the impossibility of thinking oneself out of a cubicle. The brain is an amazing thing, but it is not everything. Learning to override its desire to reduce every decision to cold, calculating, practicality is a marvelous discovery. There are deep, visceral needs that it has a tendency to brush aside, Spock-like, as irrational. By engaging the body, or the whole person, if you will, we may temporarily bypass the control center. Like an overactive dog gnawing on a bone in the corner, my brain settled on saving a dime or two in energy costs.

Thirst for connection with the natural world was ravenous. Clothespins were a means of attachment. The task morphed into the unforeseeable. Obsessed with capturing sunshine, the pastime ultimately found fruition in farming.

Orienting even a small portion of our lives around natural assets, free and abundant to all, fosters gratitude while simultaneously establishing a rhythm to our existence, one which is grounded in the real world.

A choir of songbirds transformed the space into a cathedral. Spring aromas deluged the olfactory system. Soothing sunshine warmed my back as I beheld individual pieces, feeling thankful for every item. Clothesline, adorned from end to end, became a spectacle. Wavelike billows rendered the wind visible. Senses animated, amplifying gratitude.

Such sensations are unattainable while jamming a wad of wetness into the dryer in that cold, damp space beneath one's home. Rather than a chore, laundry day is an opportunity to be thankful for the clothes on our backs.

Vivid memories arrived with every touch. A favorite pair of running socks recalled epic trips, many of which were difficult, exhausting, and discouraging. Oddly enough, those three ingredients often coalesce into delightful memories of grandeur.

One was so dreadful that I swore I'd never return to a revered spot on the Canadian border. For mystical reasons beyond comprehension, moments of sublimity among a flush of wildflowers forged a soul-captivating experience.

The socks carried me through 12 miles of Hell, becoming packed with burrs and muck. Like barnacles clinging to a ship, dozens of ticks burrowed into the wool fibers as others climbed. Always climbing! With its knee-high weeds, ankle-deep mud, and tangles of brush clawing bare legs, the run brought me to tears. At a breaking point—an otherwise healthy person can arrive at such madness that they lay down and die—I bent over in exasperation, praying I'd reach the logging road that meant smooth travel. Looking up, the old road came into view, a hundred yards down the deer trail.

All this, and more, from handling a pair of stained socks. Other articles of clothing produced their own recollections: threadbare pants, a t-shirt symbolizing a lifestyle enjoyed even as it was pursued, on and on. It seems odd to derive such pleasure from unimpressive garments. I once heard Malcolm Gladwell declare a hoarder to be, "Someone with an unusual ability to see beauty in the ordinary." Is this the final distillation of my upbringing?

On the flip side, might people over-accumulate because they don't love and appreciate their stuff enough? I love a good paradox! Unceremoniously tossing my wife's wedding dress into a soiled donation bin at Goodwill bears some irony, given this level of attachment.

Coupled with gratitude, contentment, and perspective, we can work with our flaws as lumps of clay, finding joy in slowly making them into works of art.

As laundry exhaled moisture into the atmosphere, I moved our motley crew of chicks and ducklings into the chicken tractor for their first 80-degree day outside. The feeling of grass and dirt between their toes, spindly chicken legs, and duck feet/paddles, gave them a thrill. A breeze ruffled brand new feathers, briefly exposing pantaloons. At three weeks old, they delighted in discovering rudiments of flight.

Straightforward tasks are a balm to the soul at moments of confusion. Slowing down and connecting with the world, establishing contentedness with the present, was essential for transitioning to something else.

An absurd affinity for clotheslining and chickens (turned loose from a brain that would reduce them to so many nickels and dimes) nudged me forward from a rough morning, into an alternative way of being, and even toward a fulfilling vocation. Still groping toward unexplainable intangibles, I found myself drawn toward unusual people who somehow resist that intense gravitational pull toward normalcy. Writing a book wasn't the end of the journey. Like the jettisoned fuel tank of a rocket, it merely got me off the ground. The pilgrimage was only beginning...

Act II

Close Encounters

15

I walked past his house for years, lacking gumption to knock. Charlie lived along the half-mile route that takes me to local hardware store, post office, and coffee shop. One day, while haphazardly throwing together book-launching party that would take place around the corner, I rapped on his door. Rhythmic rat-a-tat-tat opened a door to another world.

Charlie Parr is one of the most unusual and fascinating individuals I've ever met. While he wasn't available to play a few licks at my party, I encountered something far more valuable: a kindred spirit. These are about as rare as discovering a diamond. Something to rejoice in. I walked home twenty minutes later with a newfound spring in my step.

You should probably put this down and listen to every album he has put out (roots, blues, folk, old-time, soul-infused music that's deceptive in its simplicity), preferably on vinyl. Regarding online streaming, he says, "You could listen to me a thousand times on there, and I'll get about 17 cents." On another occasion Charlie says the same thing, but the number of pennies drops to 13. Observing the 25% discrepancy, I'm tempted to ask what these payments amount to, but it feels awkward. I'm endlessly fascinated by how artists get by. Even for someone of his stature, top o' the heap, it sure ain't easy.

A virtuoso with his 12-string and Resonator guitars, I'll go out on a limb and place him in the pantheon among the top 10 living country blues players in the world. I'm kind of like a boy beaming as his dad unwraps a t-shirt bearing, "World's Greatest Dad," so perhaps we should leave such rankings to cooler critics. Justin Bieber's fandom, a number approaching the tens of millions living on the entire Eastern Seaboard, dwarfs him by a factor of 343 on Spotify. A useful comparison?

The antithesis of an aloof, unapproachable celebrity, I can shake his hand and talk about the weather. This makes me love and appreciate his work all the more. Try this for yourself, by finding local musicians, artists, and writers, with whom you similarly identify.

Entirely self-taught, Parr hasn't had a single lesson. This alone might place him into the lineage of old-school folk musicians like Lightnin' Hopkins, Charley Patton, Woody Guthrie, Leadbelly, and other luminaries, but it's his life itself that renders him so bona fide.

He owes a lot to his daddy. The fist-fighting union man steeped him in soulful music. Charlie began playing on his own as a seven-year-old, showing signs of promise. The elder Parr, ever-supportive, brought him down to the music center to inquire about guitar lessons. The man behind the counter, sporting an epic mid-seventies mullet, asked young Charlie what kind of music he liked. Parr, hooked on his father's record collection, replied, "I like Lightnin' Hopkins."

"WHO??????" His dad took over at that point, lightly directed Charlie to the side, and asked the 20-something hairball,

"What kind of music do you teach?" The rocker listed off all the seventies icons you can imagine. "I can help the kid play like them." Mr. Parr politely replied, "We'll think about it." Outside, he was more emphatic. "I'm not gonna pay six bucks a lesson so you can play crap like that!"

After skipping much of his freshman year, the truancy officer was waiting for him at the door on the first day of 10th grade. "I'm going to be on you like stink on shit, Parr! You're going to come to class every day, will keep up with your homework..." In stark contrast to the vitriol, Charlie unemotionally replied, "No, I'm not." The blowhard's commands, "Get back here!!!!!" receded into the background as he walked away. He never set foot in the school again. Stubborn!

This was early '80s Austin, Minnesota, home of Spam. School had nothing for him. His father's response was remarkably laid back. He simply said, "Well, you're gonna have to get a job. I can't have you lying around here doing nothing." Staffed entirely by other dropouts, Charlie went to work at the filling station the next day. Life has been a winding road ever since.

I got to know Charlie shortly after the release of his critically acclaimed album, Stumpjumper. Recorded in an old barn, it's vintage Parr. I cherish my signed record, generously exchanged for my book. Recognizing his baggy jeans on the album cover, I asked, "Are those your only pair of pants?"

Two days later, he opened the door in pajamas.

"It's not every day the author walks up as you're finishing his book!"

Leaning from the doorway, thumb marking his place on the last page, he said, "I put Edward Abbey down to read this!"

Over tea, as his only pair of pants went through the spin cycle, Charlie nonchalantly said, "So and so understands and advocates for people like us."

Feeling accepted as sharing similar struggles and goals, I was floored. So many years in sterile environments had, "Placed my lamp under a bushel." Was I an artist?

On the heels of my exit from Cubicle Land, I craved meaningful conversations with artists like Charlie, who survive by their wits, creativity, and, what seems to the outsider like an astonishing ability to absorb risk. Being in the presence of those who appreciate and comprehend the struggle is a game-changer. There are no magic pearls of wisdom flowing from some mysterious fount. Words aren't even required. Hanging thick in the air lies an assumption, an unspoken agreement: people like us aren't meant for the office. A state of being descends, unmasked and unguarded, begetting liberation and flowering.

My place in society so elusive, I felt accepted by these people and taken in as one of them. Uncovering how they feed their families while exercising passions was a fascinating discovery. Often, it's the only thing they're fit to do. Meeting Charlie sent me down a long road of searching these people out, many of whom we'll come upon in the pages ahead.

Parr is well-established locally, regionally, nationally, and has a following in Australia and Europe, but continues to eke out a living even though he has opened for luminaries like B.B. King and Taj Mahal. Incidentally, King was warm and generous in offering him a seat at his dinner table, where they broke bread together with his band. Taj, on the other hand, made it known through an intermediary that he doesn't talk to his opening acts. Later, this same person said Taj Mahal really enjoyed Charlie's set. "He still doesn't want to talk to you," but wanted to pass along appreciation for the music. Life on the road is rarely glamorous.

When I met Charlie, he had performed 272 shows in the previous year. These pay between $200 - $450, with places like New York being on the higher end. Tours contain almost no breaks. Otherwise, traveling costs would consume profits. Charlie plays a gig, drives off to some quiet place to sleep in his vehicle, gets up for a media spot the next day, and plays a gig in the evening. By chance, I reached him by phone at an Iowa laundromat. The change in routine had perked him right up.

Once, after playing a show in Duluth, he drove down to the parking lot of a TV station in Minneapolis, where he'd be appearing on a morning show. After catching a few hours of sleep, while it was still dark, he crawled out of his vehicle looking like a homeless person. Hoping to clean up a bit, he walked into the building barefoot. At that very moment, the gorgeous host came walking around the corner. A former Ms. Minnesota, her eyes grew so wide they nearly fell out. An assistant whispered something into her ear. She recovered from her visceral reaction with a wide smile. Oh, to have been a fly on the wall for that!

A traditional job would be much safer. For one thing, he'd have a retirement plan. Parr does what he loves, is wholly devoted to his craft, but the business side simmers on the back burner. This relaxed demeanor, after fleeing a world of bean-counting and profit-squeezing, was a breath of fresh air. The approach definitely has its drawbacks, however. Charlie, some moments before taking the stage, recounts seeing hero and mentor, Spider John Koerner, tending bar. "Hey, you're on the wrong side of the bar there." Spider John retorted, "When you choose this line of work, sometimes you've got to stand on this side of the bar."

Prior to boarding a plane with the engine of his livelihood, an airline rep advises, "By handing this guitar to us, you are absolving _____Airlines of all legal responsibilities concerning the safety of this item." An act of faith...

Disembarking in Australia, guitar slides into baggage claim with a broken neck. Blood ran cold. Hours before his first show, he spread out the pieces atop a bar, as if on an ER's gurney. While puzzling over a course of action, the resourceful bartender saved the day by pulling out a box of "Icy poles." Popsicle sticks and tape held the neck together enough to get by, but since he played shows back-to-back-to-back each night of the 30-day tour, the sound deteriorated after just two performances. He took it apart every other day throughout the duration, patiently bracing and piecing things together. Lacking handlers for such necessities, he doesn't give the impression of enjoying these far-off places like a tourist.

While on tour in the States, he drove an inexpensive Kia with hundreds of thousands of miles on it, a road warrior that gave back while sipping gas at 40 miles-per-gallon. Parr eats endless 100-mile burritos, retrieving them piping hot from the engine's manifold (secured with a wire). His chariot, also a place of rest most nights, provides in every conceivable way.

The man is barefoot so much, only wearing shoes begrudgingly, it's as if his feet are the seat of his soul. Footwear seems to cramp more than just ten wiggly toes. Prior to touring full time, he was an advocate for the homeless and other downtrodden folk. The other ten digits seem equally important in creating a true hands and feet soulfulness.

Having Charlie drop by is a bit like being visited by an Old Testament prophet. Not one for appointments and such, he just shows up when you least expect it. One dreary day I was home for lunch while painting a nearby home. Feeling depressed, I looked out the window to discover him—feral hair, beard, tattered sweatshirt and jeans—approaching. The sight of his bare feet pushing pedals, arms spread wide across ridiculous handle bars of some crazy bike from the '70s, cheered my soul. He encouraged me to climb aboard the contraption. This wrought the joy of a puppy entering a bleak nursing home. A whole new perspective on life descended as I sat high and dry while riding ovals in the street like a little boy introduced to the Big Wheel. Hands splayed across three-foot-wide handlebars, paired with an erect, upright posture providing a perspective high above that of most automobiles, produced an expansive smile that lasted all the livelong day.

His bikes are quirky, like him. Another rig, with a long banana seat behind massive handlebars, feels so unusual that it's almost like you need to learn how to ride all over again. Parr doesn't believe in gears or "performance." As an avid biker myself, it's hard to imagine avoiding gears in a hilly town like Duluth. The simplicity of the arrangement reflects the rider himself. He has always been into biking, even in the 1980s when it wasn't cool. It's one of many indicators bearing witness to his refreshingly alternative way of being.

Charlie exudes this while striving to live fully in the now. He never seems to be in a hurry while enjoying a friendly visit. Fully present, he shuts off the phone. In our harried culture, consumed by technology and speed, he's an anachronistic breath of fresh air. Soulful music is a consequence of his lifestyle. Infused by spiritual imagery as his lyrics are, alongside tattered clothes hanging from a lanky frame, his persona screams John the Baptist, who similarly eschewed excesses of his age.

Prior to figuring out Instagram, hopelessly late to the party, his social media use was as old school as it gets. Access to Facebook, a tenuous mystery from conversations, came through the U.S. Mail. A volunteer, hundreds of miles away, received posts on scraps of paper and passed them along.

One day, still groping along in the depths of a midlife crisis, I stumbled upon the following comments on his page. Charlie's a master of the run-on sentence…

Folks don't just stop by the house too often, which seems a shame, I can remember my Dad's friends dropping by out of the blue just because they were in the area and they'd all sit around the kitchen table with the coffee talking about nothing in particular. Sometimes Brother Dave stops over and we throw guitar bits back and forth with the coffee, but other than that it's usually just Reuben and me bumming around the house or picking up sticks and dog poop in the yard.

Eddy Gilmore stopped over the other day, though, out of the blue, and I got so happy to see someone that I talked his ear off and nearly drove him away. Eddy's a pure soul, though, he wrote a

book called The Emancipation of a Buried Man which he left me
and I thought it was a great read so I returned the favor, dropping
out of the grey sky along with the rain into his personal home to
share tea and another round of nonstop chatter from me. Years
ago it was work for anyone to scrape a sound out of me, or even a
look, I was so shy, but nowadays I'll wear the dog out with endless
monologues concerning idle and meaningless things, things that
mean the world to me somehow. So it goes, I'm turning into a
trapdoor spider, waiting in the house for some innocent soul to
stop by so I can weave my web of dog walk incidents and daughter
hair snarls and bent tuning machines and bicycle tires and pants
that don't fit because I was too impatient to try them on at the
store. Small wonder that no one drops in.

Thank you, by the way, for all the understanding and kind words
I've been receiving lately. We're all hanging in there around here,
and I'm grateful that I'm home to help out. Reuben's doing well
and seems to be a lot happier without that kidney stone so that's
good, we walked our little route yesterday, poking our noses into
everything from shrubs to the hardware store. I talked the whole
time, telling her about my plan to get off my butt and start some
tomatoes in that nice 5 gallon bucket we found last week. Listen,
I'm gonna shut up now and see what Reuben has to say.

Can you imagine what this meant to me? Here I am, after
all, musing on it eight years later.

I'm not implying that Parr's a perfect specimen of
humanity, whom we'd all agree to offer up to visiting aliens as
an exemplar. He has publicly battled depression for years. Also,
why does he wear the same increasingly hole-riddled Austin
sweatshirt? Perhaps it has fully decomposed by now. I wouldn't
know. Since he moved out of the neighborhood, our visits have
mostly ceased. His elderly mother sends him new ones, but he
gives them away.

Gifts and money flow through him. We donated some art prints to go toward medical debt, after a shoulder-destroying accident nearly ended his career. A stream of donations exceeded his bills. He added the excess to a $20,000 donation to Life House, which serves homeless teens. At this same time, the very height of the pandemic, his income had dried up almost entirely. Disconnecting his cell phone was perhaps only the most visible step of slimming expenses down toward minimal life support. Many of us see him looking like a hobo, and naturally want him to have a bit more. He sees needs greater than his own. I suspect a retirement account is non-existent. It's kind of irritating, actually, but how can one begrudge a man of such actions. Perhaps his previous work in homeless advocacy made him allergic to money and possessions (other than records and bikes). While he's more agnostic about matters of faith than me, a Christian, he challenges me on a spiritual level. Take these lyrics from a song called, "Empty Out Your Pockets," for example:

Well, empty out your pockets, cuz here comes the Lord.
You know you can't get to Heaven, carrying all that load.
Well he's riding that little black train from glory to the ground.
When Jesus gets here, he's gonna burn that whole town down.

As a possessor of one of the fanciest theology degrees in all the land, and also a guy who has a history of obsessing about money, not only do these lyrics make me chuckle by the way he sings and lives them, they present a direct challenge.

His differentness isn't for everyone. Parr's innate otherness extends to every area of life, particularly refreshing for anyone attempting to extricate themselves from the beige sameness of Corporate America. I deeply miss our irregular visits. The loss is a vivid reminder that we need each other in our respective communities. People with wildly different perspectives on life add so much color to one another's day by day walks. It's a tragedy that in this era of unrelenting division and divisiveness around politics, that the huddled masses remain confined within their own tribes. That is remarkably boring!

Meeting Charlie sent me down a pathway to engage more intentionally with other artists, those freaks and weirdos who find ways of making a living outside the norm. My mindset would never have changed if I had followed the same well-worn path. I can hardly believe my luck in having knocked on his door when I did, when he had a bit of extra time on his hands, but only two months before his house went up for sale.

So, with that, go knock on that door in your neighborhood. The resulting experience just might change your life, but the opportunity will not stick around forever. Remember, neighbors have greater privileges than most.

16

After a morning spent with the Life House staff, whose mission is reconnecting homeless and street youth to their dreams, I raced down the hill to catch a bus. Having missed it by a few minutes, the feeling of being marooned downtown felt valuable for the story I'd write.

Cold and alone, I faced a question. Should I catch another bus that'd get me within two miles of home, and then walk the rest of the way to better identify with my subject?

Immersing myself into cold, hunger, and confusion was the intent. A biting wind roared off the Lake on a frigid March day. Mission accomplished.

As I weighed options, feeling bereft at the edge of society, a warm taphouse beckoned knowingly. Like Hansel and Gretel's bewitched gingerbread house, the pull was irresistible.

I lasted two minutes.

I could count on one hand, with fingers to spare, how

many times I've frivolously bought myself lunch and a beverage across a quarter-century.

Stepping inside, I noted sign taped to door:

_____ *Taphouse does not provide restrooms to the public. Bathrooms are private, provided for the convenience of our patrons. You may be asked to make a purchase if you want to use our facilities.*

Seating myself, I promptly received service and a warm meal, and paid with a credit card: $14.31.

That year's income placed our family well below the federal poverty line.

I was tired.

Cold.

Hungry.

An impulse purchase at a moment of weakness.

Vagabond's endurance of polar vortex—credit card, prospects, hope, all absent—is another world. Compounding things, roaming teenagers have little life experience to draw upon.

An hour apart from that relentless wind, burger and beer in hand, felt amazing. Every need attended to as an honored guest, I only rose to relieve myself.

I arrived home to junk mail advertising a pre-approved personal loan. Flyer dangled an array of temptations: dream kitchen, the ultimate vacation, the perfect wedding.

What a dichotomy. Statistics might lump my family among the poor, but we are rich in hope and love. Many kids who drop in to Life House know none of this. They are frequently survivors of sexual exploitation, and have engaged in degrading acts for the sake of spending a single night inside during sub-zero weather.

I spoke with a gal, who, at the age of four, hitchhiked with her mother from Utah to Duluth.

The state patrol picked them up in southern Minnesota. After delivering them to the bus station, the officer passed a basket to raise fare for two tickets.

Distilling everything into a coherent story for the glossy magazine was challenging, but I was fortunate. Family car was required in two places at once. Problem shape-shifted into a solution.

Rather than showing up at Life House stressed after circling blocks for a space downtown—inevitably plugging meter with three instead of four quarters, and thus damning myself to obsessing about the time—I walked that last mile. Through no virtue or prior planning, I entered the story via immersive experience. By the time I arrived at the drop-in center—steam billowing from a manhole cover in the gritty intersection—I was fully present, aware, and mentally available to sense a bit more of the soul of place and people. In short, I could connect.

Despite the lack of any grand strategy, the journey became integral to the experience. The delightful saunter carried me into forgotten history and alongside architectural gems hidden in plain sight beneath a veneer of hard luck. The sojourn itself became Memory's forge.

Perspective shifts on foot, even while passing familiar landmarks. Perambulating with an open heart and mind, upon sturdy soles, cannot help but move you. Forward, yes. But, there is movement inside that runs deeper than the bowels. Way down in that mysterious place where deep feelings and lived experience coalesce into character—a deep well of possibility—we may more fully encounter a particular corner of the world as "they" do. Just as perspective is multi-dimensional, this is far more than viewing a landscape as an amalgamation of pixels into images. Rather, the whole person is engaged: body, mind, and soul.

Writing, minuscule income notwithstanding, became a vehicle for visiting people from all walks of life. Years of earnest blog posts, columns for the free newspaper, and a book rife with flaws, imparted a badge for entering private spaces and launching into personal questions. Never one for small talk, I cherish the opportunity.

I only recall a single instance of an interview request being turned down. An impossibly elderly man paced a 3-mile stretch of Superior Street for years, hunched over and clad in a safety vest, with the aid of his walker. It seemed to take him all day. Virtually every time I hopped in the car, I'd pass by in wonderment. On a return trip, hours later, he'd still be at it!

After scoring the monthly newspaper column, I finally pulled over on my bike (homebound from Cubicle Land) to inquire about a sit-down. Immediately upon shaking his hand and catching his accent, "German Jew and World War II" flashed into my mind.

My intuition was right, but there was a twist. He agreed to tell his story. Ever the procrastinator, I called him six months later. By then, his health was failing. Walks had ceased. Reticent to attract attention to himself, Don demurred.

Later, from his widow, I learned he had escaped the Nazis and joined the British army to fight them. Afterward, he became a Quaker. The pacifist feared glorifying his past.

This story will forever be the lunker that got away. If I had only joined his walk, patiently peeled back layers and gained trust, things would have been different.

Years later, around the time of the Life House story, Blake Shippee reached out to discuss a bit of writing for his band. The fella had fallen into the habit of walking year-round to the downtown office of his property management business. Settling on a $125 commission (freelance writing quickly proved hopeless), I joined his morning walk to discuss the project: a six mile round-trip meander through run-down and passed over neighborhoods.

Though stunningly successful, Blake comes off more hillbilly than business mogul. His practice of briskly treading the pavement while chewing on thorny philosophical matters keeps him in excellent physical and mental shape. A man of unusual depth, this movement (body and mind in tandem) fosters a balanced existence. The business empire hasn't overwhelmed his creative side. Devotional observation effervesces into lyrics, musicality, rhythm.

Half a decade later, I fall somewhere on the outer edges of his periphery. Friendship lies in dormancy. Having placed boots on the ground beside him for all those miles, entering his world, granted me the privilege of burying the treasure of solidarity along the way. It sits there, waiting to be unearthed.

If I ever need a favor, and I almost certainly will, he'll be there for me. He'd probably be delighted to catch up if I called him today. I probably won't do that, though I should. Hope of friendship brings joy enough.

Serendipitously, while struggling through a draft of this very chapter, Blake called me for another commission. This time he engaged my wife's services. A stunning image now dries in her studio for the cover of his first solo album, recorded under the name Shippee. This collaboration, soon to find its way onto my turntable, is a fruit of that long-ago journey of discovery. Though his payment for the work will fund our family's existence for the next three weeks, I sit in greater anticipation of our first visit since that earlier failed commission.

Walking a mile in another man's shoes is easy. In an era of shocking divisiveness and divides, we'd do well to build more bridges. Might the solution be as simple as this?

The genesis of Life House dates to the late '80s, when Mary Robillard did just this. Her son invited a friend for a sleepover on a Friday night. When the friend didn't go home on Saturday, Mary thought, "I guess this is going to be a weekend sleepover." Sunday afternoon came and went before her son finally shared the truth. The kid had nowhere to go.

Robillard, like most of us, lacked wealth or social standing. With a little help, she founded Life House in 1991, just two years after that sleepover.

The cover story came off ok, but I'm not an effective journalist. The stories don't come naturally. I'm incapable of merely dropping in, gathering facts, and efficiently pumping out a story. I must connect emotionally by entering the subject's world. The process is so simple that I believe anyone could employ a similar strategy to connect more fully into the lives of neighbors and community.

Genuine interest in others contains power to forge friendships and bridge divides. It even helped feed my family, but not in the way I expected.

17

My compass calibrated toward beauty and simplicity early on. Stifling complexity permeated a childhood mired in squalor and family dysfunction. My heart soars in the presence of order, beauty, and intentionality. An uncommon ability to sense that which repels—meaninglessness, chaos, disorder—is a marvelous gift. These are given a wide berth. Though entropy wins its share of battles, I'm confident in the overall campaign.

Hardship in childhood enlarged my capacity for experiencing joy in unadulterated goodness. This inoculation gave rise to an unusual ability to delight in simple pleasures: those things that inject meaning into daily life. Years spent steeping in darkness and all-consuming hopelessness activated a deeper appreciation for the light. Thus, hopefulness steadily overwhelms the wasteland of want. Was I gifted a brighter future through suffering, and not merely despite it?

Day-to-day living is rarely easy. Unless my somewhat

manic alter-ego emerges, life of the party, I'm a misfit in any large group. It's common for those who grew up in similar situations to harbor the insecurities I've contended with, papering them over to blend in, while secretly tending the twin crops of bitterness and jealousy for the comparative ease enjoyed by the wealthy, beautiful, and connected. I am certainly not immune. Seeping temptation, like radon in the basement, cries injustice. Don't I deserve more?

Comparison is the thief of joy.

Virtually all of us live in greater ease and comfort than the kings and queens of lore. There is unending joy to be uncovered in our own journeys. Elemental purpose and meaning transcend artifices held in esteem by our culture and era. A gold plated toilet used by a recent President, for example, is still just a toilet.

Among a crowd, perhaps you battle insecure/jealous/bitter/carcinogenic thoughts or emotions. Dear friend, be free. You are a unique creation. No one else on earth possesses your combination of experiences and DNA. Speaking authoritatively for all humanity, we need the real you.

Not that what's inside you is necessarily right or true. Maybe you're a lost and homely mess. Excellent! Humility is the best place to start. Adventurously journeying up and out in childlike discovery offers far more than constructing normalcy's facade. An unconcealed mess is liberating. Delight in tiny victories while hacking through the jungle.

Bitterness beckons marination in acridity. In pursuit of warped pleasure, even as their humanity dissolves, the victim sinks further into the witch's brew. I've witnessed this metamorphosis at close range. Creature that emerges loses the ability to connect with others, or even the natural world.

Connection to the land, community, and a common culture rooted in local realities is an additional prophylactic. As with ancient trees, rootedness promotes flourishing.

Cast adrift upon a sea of despair, my childhood lacked moorings to community, family, the land, or spiritual underpinnings. Now, in their pursuit, I'm gifted with a rare zeal and earnestness. My attempts at a tie-in are often laughably feeble. Any success, however small, brings forth unfettered, childlike delight. Life comes together in continuum. Childhood deprivations, like some permanently charged battery, stir an uncommon sense of wonder here and now.

My plight—personal inadequacies that demand I strive ten times harder at connection than the next guy—has proven critical to success. This extraordinary effort pays off every now and again, magically. The exhilaration is akin to reaching a snowcapped summit at the height of summer. In persevering, glaring weaknesses become an unfair advantage.

In the following instance, I exchanged nine hours of effort for less than 30 seconds of tangible productive value. The results of this mismatch, 1080:1, altered the course of my life.

18

An obsession over delicious, locally grown carrots opened a portal to another world. I allotted myself one per day, each the size of a Jedi's light saber. Baking in the sun at the job site with scraped paint chips clinging to sweaty skin, I looked forward to that crisp, sweet sensory bonanza all morning, pining after the orange blast of richness the way an alcoholic longs for that next bottle. Finally, reclined beneath a tree to the tune of bees coming and going along an invisible superhighway, I savored every molecule, right on up to the smallest bits clinging to the green stem. Those delectable bites, treasured in mind and belly, carried me through the afternoon. One supremely superior carrot swelled into sustaining satisfaction. Each day's manna.

Irrational joy is a signal for exploration.

Carrots were my gateway into the local food movement. This rabbit hole, approached with Alice's innocence and curiosity, got me back onto the rails. I'd launch my own agricultural enterprise in less than a year's time. Crazy.

My enthusiasm for carrots grown by the Food Farm, a local organic operation, landed me a bit part in a Kickstarter video filmed to help fund construction of a root cellar. Since driving the car for personal interests felt like robbing the family, I opted to save $5 in gas by making the 60-mile round-trip under my own power. This absurd tightfistedness became the key to an epic day that changed me. Forever.

Eccentricities, particularly combinations thereof, are an accelerant in the quest to uncover one's giftedness.

Nine hours of strenuous effort boiled down to 30 seconds of footage. This ratio of human activity to productive use (1080:1) just might be representative of our entire lives, in terms of measurable accomplishments. The realization has the potential to spark a crisis. As for me, it's liberating. I'm freed up to play more, and not take myself so seriously. Life can be enjoyed in adventurous discovery. Ironically, by abandoning a curmudgeon's dead-seriousness, we become more impactful. Exuberance naturally radiates forth when we find joy in the journey. Jubilation spreads like a contagion.

Arriving by bicycle, as a pilgrim, opened me to appreciate subtleties of place and people. Mind, body, and soul were seasoned and tenderized throughout the arduous journey, particularly during a climb out of the Lake Superior basin that persisted a full country mile. Bearing south, after spanning Duluth end-to-end, the fully forested landscape is typical of our region. At the overlook, a bird's-eye view extends across a vast civilization of timber reaching the horizon. When would I ever arrive in the hamlet of Wrenshall and it's surrounding farm country? Without the aid of a cell phone to display mileage detail, I pedaled on in faith. I'd reach County Road 4 whenever the road brought me there, and turn right.

Pressing on, the countryside gradually turned pastoral in a rare pocket of fertility. I silently cruised beside a hayfield of verdant green. A bright red barn sat perched atop a gently rolling hill beneath a clear blue sky. Living in the northland, home to so little agriculture, I eyed the tender spring grass like a lean deer emerging from winter's starvation.

The forest slowly released its grip to a patchwork of smallholdings. Metropolitan moorings faded away. Silently riding gentle undulations, I joined a landscape of symbiosis: man and nature in a delicate dance. Finally, I bounced down Food Farm's long driveway, past an array of solar panels, and found myself in the main gathering area where several seated workers prepped seed potatoes.

Penetrating a social circle normally feels impossible. Quietly showing up with my bike and backpack gave me a leg up. I ambled over to my place (completing the ring) like a weary but confident cowboy passing through a saloon's swinging doors. Upon breaking the seal of my packed thermos, steam passed along the astonishing aroma of mulligatawny soup. Senses enlivened around the circle, like an electrical chain reaction.

I entered their world unencumbered, as if passing from spaceship through space lock without burdensome suit or oxygen tank.

The contrast was remarkable when stylish film producers stepped from automobile and crunched gravel a few minutes later. The record skipped as those same metaphorical double doors swung open.

"You're not from around here."

They'd have to overcome the barrier in other ways. Circle broke. Crew moved on to other chores. It was fascinating to observe the difference in close succession, as I stumbled into this technique of entering another's world with no exceptional abilities. My weakness became a strength by physically beating down barriers erected by an atypical brain and body (excess energy, undiagnosed ADHD, OCD, and unknowable contributors to a strange brew).

After filming my humdrum contribution—aim a camera at me and I transform into a guy thinking, "Will that contraption steal my soul?"—farming's relationship with the constraints of time peeled open wonderment. I'm a proponent of slow living because it better suits the grasping of spiritual truths, meaning, and purpose underpinning all of existence. That's all well and good for the pilgrim…

This was the first sunny day after a week of rain during the spring planting season. Busy farmers don't have the luxury of meandering through their day, as I would soon learn myself. Every step is purposeful. Crops must be planted timely, particularly when nature grants a brief window.

I felt Farmer Janaki's (pronounced John-a-key) sacrifice in sparing time to grant a tour and indulge my curiosity. We enjoyed lunch at a table he built of wood milled from trees taken from his own property.

The stunning view of the farm coming to life through the picture window stoked a longing for the bucolic.

My wife's happiness was more important than romanticized notions of country living, creating dissonance. The journey ahead brought regular contact with these idyllic places, demanding careful consideration of life's next chapter.

As member's of Food Farm's CSA, weekly vegetable boxes—an aromatic, aesthetic and nutritional bonanza— transported us to their fields. Entirely unforeseen, the pilgrimage upended our lives by catapulting me into the intersection of economy, community, and ecology.

We began with such pleasantries as his unusual name, Janaki Fisher-Merritt. Can you imagine launching a political campaign as a write-in candidate with this amalgamation of consonants, vowels, and hyphen? Any misspelling, down to the last jot and tittle, disqualified a vote. Incidentally, I missed the second t of Merritt when writing this very paragraph. Indicative of a persevering spirit, he won a spot on the school board.

Ever the ice-breaking conversationalist, I commented on his diminutive salary: just $30k distilled from a quarter-million dollars in revenue.

"Yeah, we're working on that."

The birth of his first child prompted a five-year plan to grow the business. Organic farming requires thinking years in advance. The choreography of crop rotation is enough to challenge anyone, but add in constant business decisions, equipment choices, and a myriad of details both large and small, and you discover that the person at the helm must have a good head on their shoulders. This dynamic of endless decision-making was the most surprising element of launching my urban farm a year later, but his choices are on a much grander scale. $300,000 invested into a state-of-the-art root cellar was just one of many forward-thinking approaches for growth, enabling a year-round metering out of crops.

Coincidentally, I began assembling these lines five years later. Like an irksome barnacle clinging to his story, I called him out of the blue (after years of radio silence) and asked about the farm's gross sales. He cheerfully described transitioning newly-acquired land across the road into organic production. Additional acreage, along with the large root cellar for storing the increase, grew Food Farm's revenue by 50% to $370K in 2020. A devastating hailstorm in the year of Corona resulted in fewer root crops to distribute in early 2021, a major hit to sales, but Janaki shrugged it off as, "Good enough for a year like 2020." The five-year plan played out as hoped. Income and family have expanded in tandem.

This should cause the farm's members to rejoice. A quick glance at these eye-popping numbers, while contemplating the weight of responsibility and risk shouldered by someone earning a gas station attendant's salary through occasional 100-hour workweeks, affords the briefest glimpse into his sacrifice and grit.

It's worth paying a bit more if only for the relationship between farmer and eater. A thriving rural economy, wedded to metropolis, births food security. Plentiful wholesomeness, practically in one's own backyard, holds its own besides fragile, bastardized alternatives.

I'm not expounding platitudes with the benefit of a Bay Area technocrat's fat wallet. Food is far and away our largest expense. The added expenditure makes our lives richer.

After removing abstract concepts like economic relationships and land stewardship from the equation, you're still left with superior taste, nutrition, and freshness. Are these sufficient for laying out additional funds? How about your kids actually enjoying fresh, beautiful vegetables and perhaps developing a lifelong habit of eating healthy food? Might that be worth the sacrifice? Does this sacrifice—which feels more, "Treat yo' self!" than oblation—come close to approaching the farmer's?

Your food dollars are impactful. This is the logical place for beginning a habit of buying local. As a small-time farmer who persisted for hours at the market on cold rainy days, only to see his salary cut in half because crowds shun dispiriting weather, the cheerful person handing over a ten-dollar bill fortified mental health's fraying tether.

Food Farm's carrots, and other conscientious local options, are super-premium. Since hard frosts concentrate sugars in the root, tens of thousands of pounds are harvested, cleaned, and stored at peak flavor (sometimes hours before freeze-up), requiring a team of employees. Hand-weeding is similarly laborious. Carrots are relatively simple for the home gardener, but on a large scale, per Janaki, "They're a gigantic pain in the ass."

Cheap carrots are better able to handle the rigors of mechanical harvest. The corporate food system, ever mindful of squeezing out an extra penny for shareholders, prioritizes rubbery pliability over flavor and crispness. Perhaps you've noticed that slightly bitter, metallic taste, equally present in organic options, and puzzled over how to sneak them into your kid's diet.

Those industrial carrots often shrivel up in the fridge, forgotten. (I'm not clean and pure as the wind-driven snow, after all.) My locally sourced carrots never end up in the trash. They're too good for that.

Since this isn't a book of farm wisdom, I'm only accounting for a fraction of the reason local carrots cost more than their factory-farmed counterparts. Also noteworthy, Food Farm is a diversified operation. Several dozen crops require similar intentionality, a formerly ubiquitous concept known as love and care. Locating a trusted farmer is like settling on an honest auto mechanic.

This encounter—the first of any depth with a producer of our family's food—generated insatiable hunger for connection with all our growers. A sense of affiliation is vital, for our budget's girth cannot accommodate altruism. Awareness of delightful families growing much of our food—cows, pigs, chickens, cheese, fruits, vegetables—makes it taste better. Much as a sense of smell imparts unmistakable influence over one's palate (most notable upon removal), mind and heart's bond (actual love) bestows power for enhanced enjoyment of wholesome, unadulterated food.

Adventure was far from over upon saddling up for home. I had a 30-mile ride back through the countryside, much of it downhill, and through the entire extent of Duluth. An occupied body, pumping pedals in a race against the sun, pairs with a brain lit by novel experience's bounty like fine wine to red meat. The journey, abounding in contrasts, enraptured the pilgrim on every level: physical, spiritual, emotional, intellectual. Equally essential for navigational perception, these spark-bearing aspects of humanity coalesced into a unified whole.

We are more than our brains, mere neurons propelled forward by stilts encased in meat. Nor is our essential personhood expressed as a disembodied soul. The whole person is more capable of perceiving overwhelming abundance and beauty. Inherent strengths and weaknesses work together, hand in glove. By healing rifts and refusing the bifurcations of modernity, these united aspects of life may more adequately propel us forward in joy. The brain-gut connection gives credence to a literal understanding of gut feelings. Even if you don't believe in the bodily resurrection, as I do, the very existence of this time-transcending belief exquisitely articulates the joining of physical and spiritual.

This sense of expanded perception, penetrating into the depths of reality, calls to mind my first contact with the Grand Canyon. At the rim, hundreds upon hundreds of tourists were in tears or near-rapturous religiosity. For me, it was little more than a snapshot. Sullen and disappointed, my first step wasn't descent into this wonder of the world, but to a payphone, so I might shorten my stay from seven days to five. An effortless shuffle had carried me from a bus to one of the most photographed viewpoints on Earth. Only discerning dust and rock, beauty's antenna was retracted.

But, after expending myself inside the canyon—sweating, exerting, sleeping, eating, feeling—I found myself back on the Rim savoring homemade canned venison. I had reascended the Bright Angel trail with a new friend who produced a heavy Mason jar from his pack, a full quart of sumptuous chunks heated over a camp stove in a secluded spot near the edge. Here's my reaction at the same overlook, taken from the "Emancipation" portion of my book. I'll beg some forgiveness, as author Mary Karr declares, *There's a special place in Hell for authors who quote themselves.*

We sat three feet from the steep cliff in a scene of majesty.

We were part of the sublime heavenly setting. This wasn't just an overlook anymore. My DNA was left in the canyon, and a part of the canyon was in me. It was as if the deer had been sacrificed and was now being offered as a sweet-smelling burnt offering to the Maker of the Grand Canyon.

With all senses and neurons collaborating in apprehending the present, anxieties about the past or future melt away. Preternatural perception plumbs the depths of the here and now with acute discernment. Minor setbacks roll off like water on waxed canvas. Like a computer finally unburdened from the weight of unnecessary programs operating in the background, the current moment's exquisite simplicity comes into relief as all those disparate functions of mind/body/soul merge in collective abandonment of their tug-of-war.

While pedaling through an unvarnished city-scape, a stray pterodactyl's bomb bay doors opened with astonishing precision. An enormous quantity of excrement dropped from the heavens into my lap. The splatter zone encompassed the entire front of my shorts. Another first, I could only laugh.

Everybody poops.

Arriving home at dusk from the farm, I emerged from a well-earned shower as something wholly other after stepping back through the portal into a newly expanded world.

19

A brain bent toward obsession, properly screwed into the body and all its sensations, isn't necessarily a liability. Like SETI's array of telescopes and antennas aimed into space, I directed this superpower toward connecting with artists, farmers, the land, local economy, and history. Newspaper column and blog became vehicles for feeding a growing addiction. How do other weirdos make it in this world? What value might I offer my neighbors beyond simple friendship?

Desperate to explore further, I conjured up a three-day stay at Food Farm as writer-in-residence. The farming lifestyle had always captivated my imagination, but I pushed away those yearnings as childhood fantasy. Wrenshall's powerful tractor-beam pulled me in, crashing through that wall of realism.

In exploration, a full-on pilgrimage in my case, overthinking is anathema. Obsessions leave bread crumbs all the way down a rabbit hole. One never knows where they might lead. Attempts at divining a destination, or any possibility of monetary reward, torpedos a journey before it gathers steam

An ever-increasing number of CSA's carpet-bomb Duluth through weekly drops of vegetable boxes. CSA = community supported agriculture. With Food Farm as an entry point, I plumbed this world to the very bottom of my interest level, eventually securing a part-time job as farmhand.

From a vintage camper planted in the woods, I eased my bike onto country roads—marinading in the idyllic atmosphere—en route to a neighborhood of intrepid young farmers who all started from scratch. None of them had much money, but were making it happen through courage and indefatigability. GRIT! Even Janaki, born on the Food Farm, wasn't handed this life. Two inches taller than Abe Lincoln and a basketball star at a selective college, he could have picked something easier and more lucrative. In order to "inherit" the farm, he took on a large mortgage to pay for it. The land was his parents' retirement plan.

While Janaki arguably had a leg up, mainly through a childhood desensitized to hard work, how do people like me with zero experience and no money make a go at it? Isn't it impossible?

All three of the folks I met in this funky hamlet were in this category. Catherine Conover, like me, found herself deeply unhappy in jobs that didn't suit her after college and graduate school. She reached her crossroads at 29. Rather than kick the can down the road, as I did, she faced the nagging question of what to do with her life head on. All she knew was that she wanted to be outside. Feeling she had nothing to lose, and possessing an adventurous spirit, she tested the waters by securing a low-paying farm internship.

After arming herself with knowledge gained from three years of intensive work spent growing vegetables for other farmers, including a stint at Food Farm, she gained confidence to take the plunge by investing in her own land. Catherine built her CSA, Stone's Throw Farm, from scratch. When I dropped in back in

2015, she had 55 members. Full shares went for $500. #dothemath

Her sacrifice and determination is impossible to exaggerate. She didn't purchase a farm—insert farmer here—but bought 40 acres of mostly wooded, undeveloped land. A well was drilled first thing, greenhouses were erected, and then a single outbuilding. When I arrived IN YEAR SIX, she was reveling in the luxury of a newly-built bathroom. Outhouse transformed into museum piece.

Everything had to be built, systems developed, etc, while simultaneously learning how to run a business. Having gone through a fraction of this while establishing Tiny Farm Duluth in the years that followed, I'm in awe of her persistence in enduring a thicket of complexities.

Everything is boot-strapped. Unlike the 10-foot-high behemoth circumnavigating Food Farm like a penitentiary, Catherine's fortifications aren't impenetrable. Her deer fences, augmented by poles cut from her own woods, have a homespun quality. These angle outward with individual wires stretched across, as if fending off marauding vikings. Since the barrier can be jumped, she trains the deer to fear electrified wires by baiting them with peanut butter each spring.

All her farm infrastructure is similarly cobbled together with ingenuity, wit, and perseverance in the face of a challenging environment. While touring a small greenhouse converted from an old garage hoop building picked up for a hundred bucks, she described keeping seedlings heated to a miserly 33 degrees. Observing my incredulousness, she said, "Only the toughest plants survive spring at Stone's Throw Farm!"

Catherine can't afford to be wasteful.

Though the operation is compact—three acres under rotational cultivation within a seven-acre clearing—the task was gargantuan for one person to choreograph all the weeding, seeding, planting, irrigation, harvesting, packing, and more, completed largely by hand or with simple implements. Task list extends itself ad infinitum until Fall's merciful killing frost. The budget didn't provide margin for a part-time employee until her seventh year.

She was blessed by the presence of POOFs, however, which Wrenshall has in abundance: Parents Of Organic Farmers. Hers purchased a nearby summer house, donated old equipment from their farm, and regularly lent a hand.

Her accommodating significant other, Elden, was then living and working in the city. Catherine took up spartan quarters in the outbuilding several days each week in a small bedroom walled off from tools and equipment. I had arrived unannounced, quietly on a bicycle, as a weird journalist/blogger/writer-in-residence/farm enthusiast. The introvert opened doors to this inner sanctum as if they were the Crown Jewels. Bed was neatly made with crisp hospital corners. Modern bathroom shined, spotless and beautiful. Conover's countenance radiated pride and satisfaction in these finer things of life.

I got the sense that life could be more comfortable for them both if Catherine's need to farm wasn't pathological. Did her hourly earnings approach minimum wage?

Six years later, I awkwardly claimed a seat outside her home at a picnic. Beside us were two coolers of premium beer, grass clipped to perfection, and nary a weed within tidy farmscape. The atmosphere was idyllic as the sun quietly descended, leaving everything and everyone aglow. Mosquitos, in deference to perfection, buggered off to more hapless warm-bloods, causing me to wonder at her reaction to, "You're so lucky to live here."

I envy her decisive act in shifting gears before turning 30. The immense expense and time devoted to higher education was a sunk cost rooted in a teenager's limited understanding. Rather than remaining mired in soul-sucking work because of these expenditures—time and money consigned to oblivion—she forged an alternative.

I was 38 at the time of my departure—but had been 29 at the same employer—had a mortgage, kids, etc. Catherine and Elden have no children.

Radical change in favor of greater meaning and purpose is possible with kids, however. Scott Clifton abandoned the lucrative field of aeronautical engineering at 29 to become executive director of Farms International. This small and nimble non-profit provides loans to the poor in 13 countries around the world, enabling individuals and families to similarly build sustainable lives in work that suits them. Scott had three young kids (and now four), but found the courage to leave a vocation that sapped him. His family stepped forward in faith while earning half the money, fewer benefits, AND he must fundraise.

That nagging feeling of discontent in your 20s is a shot across the bow. Like a fire working its way down a coal seam, it'll smolder a hundred years.

Northern Harvest Farm is situated across the road from Catherine's smaller operation. Rick and Karola Dalen pushed their farm aspirations forward immediately after graduating college. Their farm's genesis traces back to 1.5 acres borrowed from Food Farm in 2005, enough to supply 30 weekly boxes. In a swap for land, equipment, and guidance, they served as interns at the established farm for two years. Rick worked three full days, and Karola put in two for Food Farm each week. The rest of their time—ALL OF IT—went into establishing their own farm business. Knowledge and experience accumulated across two exhausting growing seasons. Since the unusually compatible couple didn't hate the work, they took the plunge by purchasing their own land. Apprenticeship, literal attachment, is worthy of careful reflection.

They've built the farm slowly and sustainably, careful not to get in over their heads. He estimated a bottom-line profit of $15,000 in the previous year, 2014. And yes, they have kids. Karola was into her third year of full-time employment with the county, greatly easing financial concerns. After subjecting Rick to a barrage of money questions, however, there's little doubt they could have solved the puzzle of funding a family in the absence of conventional employment.

Each of these farmers has their own gifts, quirks, and foibles. Upon entering his barn, it's apparent that Rick is steadily achieving the balance he seeks. Every tool, implement, and piece of equipment has a place. Everything is in its place. As redolent as fresh air, I picked up on this immediately. Rick's barn is the most spotless I've ever seen. Also, most days he's in for supper at 6 pm sharp. Karola is a stickler. He rests content over the day's accomplishments.

In stark contrast, I sat around starving in my trailer at the Food Farm for hours that evening. Finally abandoning any pretense at writing, I stared out the window in disbelief as Janaki made repeated passes on the tractor long after sunset. Dusk passed into night. Now he'd have to bring in ol' Bessie.

Nope!

He switched on the lights and kept going.

Janaki says, almost in a tone of reverence, "Rick is a damn good farmer."

Even though it was a crazy time of year when a pause might be warranted, Rick faithfully continued his daughter's piano lessons each week. Dalen, a music minor in college, strives to pass this passion on to his children while preserving a steady presence in their lives. He says it's critical to maintain an unbroken chain of practice during the busy seasons. I wholeheartedly agree. It's far simpler than breaking the chain, and facing gargantuan task of rebuilding the habit later.

Previously members of their CSA, we dropped out a couple years in. We were a young, struggling family ourselves, and a 2012 flood devastated their work. Weekly boxes were a bit thin after large portions of fields washed out. I hadn't established a personal connection beyond a basic love for high quality produce. Life was crazy with our rambunctious twins, so we skipped the member picnics. As farmers who focus primary effort on building living soil, requiring years of thoughtful work, they experienced an enormous depletion in a single day. This gut-wrenching loss ultimately produced growth via enrollment in the school of hard knocks.

It was incredibly awkward to contradict Rick when he casually expressed appreciation for our enduring membership. The mixup was probably responsible for my all-access pass to his lunch hour. Time is at a serious premium during a farm's setup phase, particularly for a guy like Rick with fixed start and stop times.

His philosophy and spiritual practices, essentially Buddhist, are a challenge for the Christian writing these lines. He begins each day in meditation for a full hour, burning perfectly good daylight. Having an awareness of his bottomless to-do list, this blows my mind. There's major pressure to get all the work in. Consequences extend far beyond the average person's annual review. In contrast to Rick's unusual discipline, and though I presume to converse with the author of all things, I struggle for five minutes of devoted, undistracted prayer. Rick puts in a full 60 every day, and this in the absence of any firm belief in God. Might there be something I could learn from him?

Local food, grown by families on the periphery of cities, is probably the simplest gateway toward healing our fracturing society. Maybe, just maybe, we could declare an armistice in the culture wars and focus on the 80% of practical issues that provide common ground. These people sacrifice comfort and bear otherworldly risk and stress out of love for their communities.

Even matters involving diverging worldviews, such as Rick's early practice of relocating pests like potato bugs (practicing nonviolence) are amusing topics for conversation and wonderment. How can a farmer succeed without killing pests? Has he rationalized death by now? Perhaps one of his members will ask.

Risking language connoting the use of chloroform, pins, and foam, Rick is a remarkable specimen. He and his beautiful family are exemplars of humanity. But, since you're probably not a farm nerd like me, nor an alien with a growing collection, I must move on to an individual I met by chance at Northern Harvest. Adam Kemp was then in his 8th year as a farmhand in 2015. He commanded the princely sum of $11.75 an hour. Rick, who wished he could pay twenty, was bringing home a shave less. Compare this to your wage (double it to account for vacation pay, health, dental, and retirement), and ponder the likelihood that you feel underpaid. I certainly resented 2% raises each year as beneath my contribution. Not only is Adam not bitter about the relationship, he purchased land directly across the street from his job!

He was in the earliest stages of developing a berry farm, focused on rebuilding marginal soil, and shacked up in a two-car garage with his wife and one-year-old child. Slowly, methodically and sustainably, Adam and his wife built a lifestyle and farm: Uff-da Organics. After adding a second child, they remained in the garage for several more years. Drip by drip, nest egg grew. With the patience of an oak, they waited.

And worked.

Yesterday, seven years later, I raced into this space while struggling with a zipper. Tripping over a four-inch step elevating room above cold concrete, finding the bathroom (the only partition within an open floor plan) wasn't difficult. Was there any sanity in here with toddlers climbing all four walls?

As if delivered by spaceship, a modest modular home dropped onto the property in 2020. To them, it's Versailles.

Building an alternative lifestyle from scratch—much like transforming a loose collection of molecules coalesced as dirt into a thriving population of organisms working in concert as living soil—requires patience and sacrifice wholly alien to modernity's fetish for instant gratification. The consent, cooperation, and wholehearted commitment of the entire family are prerequisites.

Very few people can pull this off. We must invest in them. The loss, if they fail for lack of support, is incalculable.

I've been returning to Uff-da with my family these past few years, where we pick strawberries presidentially. Adam schedules one group at a time. Instead of long lines and crowds, we have the field to ourselves. It's as if the Secret Service has cordoned the place off for POTUS. We leave with 25 pounds of perfectly ripe organic berries, many of which are frozen for enjoyment in winter. Gobs of free strawberries skip the middleman altogether, descending straight into bellies for processing. Clean, pesticide-free strawberries sell themselves. They're perfect for a grower like Adam, who, with his shy and unassuming Farmer Brown manner, is the prototypical anti-salesman.

Bucking the trend toward financial independence, these families strive for interdependence. Their sacrifice and grit in pursuit of wholesome ideals should inspire us all.

There was morning and there was evening, connections betwixt. Surfaces barely scratched, I returned to Food Farm in joyful overflow, and churned out a couple thousand words until those tractor lights switched on. Hunger and exhaustion overwhelmed idealism, relentless as Alexander's armies sweeping across Mesopotamia.

Tractor finally silenced, I joined Janaki and his wife in the main house after counting to a thousand.

"Do you always eat supper at nearly 10 pm?"

"Oh, this is early!" came the unanimous reply.

Awash in vegetables—carted away in thousand-pound increments—their own nourishment is an afterthought.

Following a lively conversation, I turned in and caught Janaki watering the turkey chicks at 10:30 pm. Romantic lifestyle, indeed.

Blessed with a newborn, they were fortunate to have his parents (who live in a separate home on the property) assist with childcare. Annie's parents, joining POOF rank and file, purchased a nearby home as well. They've added an additional child since then. I suspect these late night marathons have abated a bit, but I suppose finding balance will be a lifelong growth area. Growing a family adds a wrinkle for the driven.

Janaki's wife, Annie Dugan, grew up in wildly different circumstances. Rather cosmopolitan, she deftly wields a Master of Arts degree from Columbia University in daily life. Before agreeing to move to the sticks and marry Janaki, she had three conditions:

1. Delivery of the New York Times
2. Access to high-speed internet
3. Reliable cell phone reception

Though she conceded for a spell by biking to the Carlton library for email access, all arrived in short order as a cosmic gift. Annie was serving as the Executive and Artistic Director of the Duluth Art Institute, where my wife's breakout art exhibition would soon go on display. Unencumbered by big girl credentials—I picture her toning them down on a resume—

she remains highly approachable. Dugan comes alive through fostering connections between others, standing back, and simply appreciating whatever sparks may fly.

On the day I inquired about staying at their farm as a writer-in-residence, a nebulous notion, I arrived unshaven and sweaty at her downtown office immediately adjacent to a white-walled art exhibit. She was friendly, thoughtful, and vivacious. In short, engaging. Happy to see me, eager even, Annie purchased my book at full price. She welcomed me as a fellow creator/artist, someone uniquely valuable. I was a schmuck whose book sales crept up one or two at a time, married to a then-unknown artist, but she described us as a power-couple.

Annie saw diamonds in all that duff. Like a respected art connoisseur who discovers an eccentric artist in the hollers of Appalachia, she applied mysterious catalytic powers.

These eyes, capable of seeing beyond the surface and admiring innate talent, are powerful. In exercising this vision, we might even mend society's deepest rifts. At the very least, their healing waters worked wonders in me.

In entering this couple's story, I sank roots into our area's rich agricultural and art worlds, a scene growing richer in the fullness of time.

Culture is a bounty as ubiquitous as radio waves. We need only tune in.

A community loses its identity if it cannot produce much of its own art, entertainment, food, or express appreciation for manifest beauty.

Straightforward enjoyment of culture, like a child's craving for that next lick of ice cream, is infinitely more satisfying and productive than the bunker mentality fueled by culture wars. We conserve through consumption.

In consuming, we become participants ourselves.

20

It's difficult to conceive of a more potentially mismatched couple than Janaki and Annie. Her prerequisites for country living are tips of an iceberg. Fresh ideas, community engagement, and culture on the leading edge are deep-seated needs firmly entrenched in her soul's bedrock. A 30-inch stack of Times art sections testifies beside the picture window and its bucolic view.

To make life sustainable on the farm, she ushers city into country, deftly maintaining feet in both worlds. The Free Range Film Festival, set within a gorgeous old barn, is one of many synergies to spring up at the collision point.

Annie, now an art history instructor and independent curator who provides "limited weeding services," commutes to Duluth for her day job. Having observed her as a closeted introvert, rural living must be a bonanza for private life. Tying herself to the land also adds stability. Unlike her cohorts, who typically leap from one lily pad to the next in a quest for more impressive titles, she must navigate the limited opportunities of this place. In remaining—committing—Dugan has become an indispensable lynchpin.

Far from impedimental, as long as there is room to run, wildly different expressions of giftedness are a boost to personal and marital satisfaction. The latter largely depends on the former, in fact. Those who control or squelch their spouse's disparate interests are missing out on a more interesting existence.

My lot in life is the inverse of Annie's. Her retrofitting of life and place are a model for the odd duck. Rather than seasoning the rural with urbanity, I'm endeavoring to escort agrarian living into the city.

If it weren't for a series of blunders, a life lived in tandem with a large tract of land may have been a possibility earlier on. A disastrous stint at a rural retreat center is chief among them. After leaving the stimulating environment of graduate school in the Boston area, this country spot was far too isolating with its provincial attitudes. Conversational red flags went unheeded, and then I declined an offer to fly out and see the place.

After piloting a moving truck 1500 miles into the heartland, an overwhelming sense of foreboding fell upon me as we trundled up the long driveway. A vast fleet of rusting machinery and equipment on the hilltop spoke volumes. I should have apologized profusely and reconnoitered elsewhere. Instead, we unpacked the truck with Shawna's parents, handed them the keys, and were left behind. Trapped. I knew this was a grave mistake from the moment we arrived, but fulfilled the one-year commitment to the very day.

Every time I have gone against such a strong gut feeling, I've regretted it. Once again, the gumption required for a young person to assert him or herself among elders is extraordinary. Prior navigational challenges involved things like selecting a course of study, rarely requiring a hard turn of the wheel.

A clear understanding of what repels you can be as valuable as any degree.

The other unforced error was remaining cubicle-bound for 12 soul-sucking years, a shipwreck if there ever was one. Failing to pay heed to that feeling in the gut has consequences. Thus, my context deviated significantly from that of those farmers I so admire.

As the family's sole breadwinner, I wasn't able to sacrifice in the same ways. Transitioning in midlife is a different kettle of fish. None of this really matters, however, because Shawna became unwilling to relocate. An introvert, she fears she'd wall herself off in isolation. Our kids are also in their last lap of high school. The window for moving our family out onto the land has closed. Years flew by as we subsisted in survival mode. Like some deliciously hoppy IPA, should I indulge in bitterness?

Heck no! While I'd adore stewarding 40 acres, that lifestyle isn't my entire world. Is that all I'm living for? Of course not! I love God, family, and neighbor more. Much more. Also, there's this annoying feeling that I'm not as suited for such a life as I might think. Circumstances appear to have been steered providentially against it. Joining the flow, rather than fighting it, is a place of rest and security.

Since I'm choosing against blowing up our lives and becoming a bitter old man in the country, I'll bring as much wildness and rural ways into the city as I can. And where I fall short, well, I'm only human. Ultimate dreams and goals transcend smaller ones like this. Finding thrill in the chase is key. Enjoy the journey, all the while knowing you'll never arrive.

Rather than bemoan a wife who differs from me, daily flashes of her essential otherness (beauty, love of beauty, artistic brilliance, quirky sense of humor, compassion, and so much more) are reminders of what drew me to her in the first place. Shawna's unique take on the world blows my mind, attesting to completion. Collective wholeness.

It's helpful to have found a mate who not only supports my goals, but delights in them. We brim with joy when the other soars in discovery or exercises passions in new or unexpected ways. The launching of my urban farm, for example, prompted a marvelous painting called Big Dreams. I'm glad it hasn't sold. Perhaps it'll revert to the original title: Eddy's Overwhelmed. Rather simple and childlike, a small boy hoists a daisy five times larger than himself before a starry backdrop. The weight and beauty of that flower linger on. Her imprimatur in the bottom corner, Gilmore, is an endorsement (or blessing, mayhap). Let it so be...

Concurrently, she created another piece that must reflect the other side of the coin. Unfortunately, She Saw It Coming, has more universal appeal. It sold for a paltry $225. If only it could hang side by side with the other, but we were starved for cash. Shawna swears this painting isn't about us, but she's clearly crazy. Man and woman in '40s vintage attire, lovers apparently, sit in a picturesque field of daisies. He's leaning in and smiling optimistically, oblivious to the raging forest fire in the distance. This piece bubbled up from her subconscious after I described my plan to launch an urban farm on other people's land. It's perfect.

I'll never take it for granted, but always expected society to endorse her work. She has skills, talent, and imagination that are wholly other. Sitting back and resting in this requires no virtue or "Husband of the Year" material.

Her content is always surprising—the very opposite of predictable—much like her income. We invested over a thousand dollars in supplies last week, a lot to chew on after sales had dwindled down to the occasional inexpensive print. Then, after ordering ink, paper, panels, and random crap that accumulate into serious expense, Shawna spent an entire day crafting a newsletter that reaches a couple hundred people. I thought she was crazy, but connecting with her peeps brings her joy, so I focused on my own work. Five minutes after sending out her email, a collector in Los Angeles (some newscaster on the teevee) snatched up a $4200 painting. Not only will this pay for those supplies, it should cover our upcoming trip to Montana. Amazing!

By simply allowing Shawna space to run wherever whimsy carries her, wonderment invariably follows. And, to clarify, this "allowance" has nothing to do with male/female dynamics. It's incredibly easy for either party in a partnership to stamp out impracticality, like some annoying brushfire. Subtle notes of disapproval, or harping to get out there and kill something to eat, are equally effective.

Like salt, a dash of healthy skepticism does ya fine.

Incidentally, this trip West will be our family's second road trip. The first, a journey south four years ago, was paid in full when four paintings sold all at once the day before we left. A joyful wave of astonished gratitude carried us through a spring snowstorm all the way to ocean's distant shore, where blossoms had opened that day.

Four beating hearts swelled with faith, enriched and renewed.

Money had previously been a dominating character in our family's story. Now, in contrast, we concentrate on the work itself, serving our customers as partners in life, and living joyfully. Gratitude is a natural byproduct, as is life-sustaining income. Money flows into our well, from some inexhaustible aquifer, almost automatically.

Simple forward progress, inch by painstaking inch, builds a household economy. We've transformed into two horses, relaxed while hitched to the team, equally pulling the load. The beauty in the arrangement is that we can each make tough choices that exact a temporary economic cost, such as sacrificing thousands of dollars for a massive influx of time by cutting out the twice-weekly farmers market, for long-term sustainability.

Our goals don't include achieving fame, building careers,

or becoming business juggernauts. We're pursuing a form of financial independence (intertwined within our community so perhaps interdependent is more accurate) while crafting lives suitable to our family's unique rhythm. Following years of struggle, we've finally found freedom for work that brings us joy, and thus has the greatest impact.

A season of 100-hour workweeks darting across creation to different farming locations proved unsustainable, so I whittled the farm down to the bare minimum to prevent burnout, creating space for writing, while providing for our family's basic needs. I admit it's not quite enough for comfort, or to contribute meaningfully to a retirement plan, but this lack lights a fire beneath us.

All three legs of our financial stool might seem nonsensical by themselves. When understood as one cohesive whole, however, they fit together sturdily. Our support for each other isn't passive. It's active! This is one household economy, rather than a collection of competing interests. Failure is a surety if we succumb to petty self-interest.

Shawna grants me space for this insane drive to write books, and provides critical support by packing individual clamshells of microgreens. She designs labels and has crafted playful farm propaganda pieces, such as "Lettuce Is Relaxing," and "Veggies Make You Strong."

I support Shawna's work by handling bookkeeping, invoicing, keeping galleries stocked, etc. Humdrum business tasks fall outside her skill set, so I do what I can to liberate the creative force so vital to our wellbeing. Her current paintings are far more captivating than anything described here, by the way.

Synergy is mysterious. The combined effect of our efforts is greater than the sum of its parts. We each have glaring weaknesses, but together we're fortunate to build a lifestyle fitting to our unusual personalities. Individually, we'd never succeed.

Building a life is more satisfying than buying that farm.

While I've made serious compromises, it's helpful to sense Shawna's intransigence as a positive check upon my impulsiveness. She has provided limits within which I may work, while also sparing us from crushing debt.

The problem—Shawna tethering us to a 50 X 140-foot city lot—is the solution. Limits, far from detrimental, frame life's canvas. They define the space for unleashing creative potential.

A 40-acre canvas is probably too much for my limited abilities. Yielding to realism, even when imposed, is liberating. Better to leave something romanticized than taste its fruit and find it bitter.

Like a grandparent unburdened by all the struggles, I enjoy the country by maintaining relationships with nearby farmers. Carrying home so many boxes is my equivalent to dragging home an animal, but without the work.

These friends, and their sacrifice, come to mind with every bite of grass-fed beef, whenever a frozen strawberry releases summer's goodness into wholesome hot cereal during a snowstorm, or with the sound of a crisp carrot arriving at its destiny through mastication. The land, broken down into molecules, transfers into my DNA. Even something as banal as collecting manure at a nearby stable—fertility carried home in buckets for a garden experiment—scratches this itch.

My insatiable thirst for the land includes adventuring upon it, another key difference between us. Sha-nay-nay is up for the occasional family romp, but an entire afternoon spent traversing 16 miles on the Superior Hiking Trail doesn't turn her crank. Hours of movement, harnessing brain and body, are imperative for my wellbeing. Having the liberty to press on, usually solo, makes me a better husband and father.

Kryptonite for the Bahamian beachgoer, my ideal winter vacation includes hours of struggle through several feet of snow in pursuit of a primitive shack perched within a stone's throw of Canada. Dense forest girds these mid-latitudes, stretching north as far as a little plane will travel. While the waters demarcating this border spot rush toward Lake Superior, a very short portage (carry of the canoe) crosses the continental divide at the edge of this particular watershed. Those waters head north to Hudson Bay, where this vast forest gives way to tundra. Even now, my heart skips a beat.

Shawna has no such longing.

Hardcore adventure helps me function properly. This pushing of mind and body exorcizes addictive tendencies that might otherwise dismantle our marriage brick by brick. Everybody pays when I'm not getting enough: arguments, micro-managing the kids, stressing over money, etc.

At the height of the pandemic, I slipped away to the Boundary Waters Canoe Area Wilderness for three glorious fall days. I begged Team Gilmore to join me, for a popular entry point affording easy access to Rose Lake—perhaps the crown jewel of border country—was available. Incredibly, nobody wanted to skip school.

Rather than sulk, as I've done in the past, I invited a friend instead. Since I barely see the fella anymore, it was a total Hail Mary pass. Our friendship rekindled, and we had the experience of a lifetime.

Locking in the trip by paying the $38 fee was an electrifying commitment. The best investment I've made in years, my dominating facial feature in the hellscape that was the latter half of 2020, was a permanent grin.

Rose Lake is nestled within the most impressive topographical features on offer in the Midwest. Nearby cliffs, a natural redoubt at the edge of our national jurisdiction, afford awe-inspiring views of wilderness lakes typically reserved for the covers of calendars. Tourists were notably absent, shaken off the picnic blanket like pesky ants. Even the mosquitoes granted the courtesy of dying off before our arrival, as we enjoyed all this abundance under bluebird sunny skies.

Joy, wonder, and gratitude remained with me long after the vacation ended. A few days after returning home, some roving pack of bastards cut out the catalytic converter under our Prius. Thinking it might be a couple hundred dollar inconvenience, I called the repair shop to get a jaw-dropping quote of $2300. This minor disaster rolled off me like water, even before figuring out the complex task of having insurance cover all but $500. Life is full of unexpected disappointments. Sailing into them with a healthy mindset makes all the difference in the world.

Wife and kids enthusiastically support these endeavors, because we all benefit through a sense of overflowing joy. Conversely, we suffer when even one of us lurches through life unfulfilled, particularly at such times as pandemic-era quarantining. Each of us must continually engage in challenging activities enlivening to brains and bodies. This is fuel and lubrication for the four-cylinder engine that is our household economy.

In choosing self-employment, one is no longer faced with justifying major expenditures of time. Decade-spanning success comes to those who intuitively act without regard for appearances to anyone outside the family unit. Marry the right person and this shouldn't be difficult. Relationship is increasingly awash in delight as either party thrives. When they light up, so do you.

In piloting a single household economy, we eschew all notions of competing career goals. This is a three-legged stool: art, farm, written word. Each supports and overlaps the others. There are no clear boundaries. I sold art prints and books alongside veggies at the farmers market, for example, and paintings have a way of finding a home through a snapshot shared by Tiny Farm Duluth on Instagram. Customers organically wayfind to all three points of our compass.

There have been no home runs, but we're consistently making base hits. We've learned that long-coveted bits of media exposure, though welcome, have small incremental effect. Therefore, we aren't desperate for attention anymore, which ironically should make us better radio, podcast, and television guests in the future. We've done them all, particularly Shawna, who sees a handful of inexpensive art prints shipped afterward. While disappointing at first, this realization frees us to focus on the work. There is no gatekeeper upon a white horse to carry us through pearly gates of fame and fortune.

The work whispers. Those with ears to hear will hear.

A few miles away, in a place of joy, an entire wall is consumed by Shawna's imagination. Untold thousands, all patiently waiting for the area's best artisanal ice cream, are charmed by it. On rare occasions, the experience sweeps new business our way. Mostly, however, it simply brings a smile and a trace of wonder. Mission accomplished.

Our work places us inside the dynamic, ever-shifting stream of civilization's output and tastes. Just as this mural is off to the side, a delightful surprise for tourists on the hunt for something delectable, my farm's limited offerings often find themselves in a lovely pile beside the main course, dressing up a hamburger or sandwich, or adding beauty to a chef's creation. Becoming the main course is no prerequisite to happiness or fulfillment, nor are prospects for remuneration. Showing up, joining the conversation and contributing to culture's flowering, is both satisfying and sustainable. For a lifetime.

21

A castaway seeking mooring, I thirsted for contact with mortals living life itself as an expression of art. Instead of compartmentalizing personal passions into little cubes and packing them away, these stouthearted souls reject modernity's bifurcations: work vs private life, sacred vs secular, etc. Our giftedness, cultivated to flower, is humanity in bloom. The corporate world, for the sake of standardization and producing predictable widgets, mows one-of-a-kind potential down to the ground. It's not personal. Cut grass is manageable. A field of wildflowers? Not so much.

A scarcity mindset was my underlying disease. Though I lacked this terminology, the quest became a search for an antidote. Perhaps originating in childhood poverty, this limited way of being was reinforced while toiling for highly regulated companies where the prevailing tendency was the covering of one's backside. Raises were minuscule. Promotions few. Grinding efficiencies dispelled creativity.

While subsisting in scarcity, one fears failure like Smaug the dragon. Anxiety is ubiquitous. Risk-taking, unimaginable. Dare not lose the little bit you already have.

Descending to the bottom rung as a neophyte, I sought encounters with people wielding creative gifts, grit, perseverance, and abundance mindsets. By ENCOUNTER, I'm referring to the way one might stumble upon a bear in the woods or have a brush with a force of nature beyond control or understanding, a once-in-a-lifetime moment with power to alter your trajectory. Big Head Ed couldn't think himself through the thicket.

Adam Swanson is somehow immune to scarcity. He's a member of a loose collection of painters I call The Rat Pack, a handful of our area's most accomplished artists who gather to critique and spur one another on. Shawna's work has grown deeper and richer through her participation. These are fascinating individuals, square pegs unfit for the well-worn path. Trailblazers.

Swanson is insanely prolific, producing in excess of 150 paintings a year. He is also more active in the public art space than virtually any other being, aside from The Lord. His murals, massive creations spanning hundreds of square feet, burst forth like a flush of mushrooms across the forest floor. A personal favorite adds incredible color to an exterior brick wall of the Grand Rapids Area Library. In his photo taken after installation, Adam stands before the creation with an understated Mona Lisa-like smile of satisfaction, arms hanging casually at his side. An enormous chickadee dwarfs the artist. A normally diminutive bird, it consumes about half of the 500 square foot painting. An active family in the background is life-sized, amidst a scene punctuated by generous flourishes of color. Bird's eye, larger than Adam's head, peers out on the world, quietly urging us to consider the impact of our actions.

Humanity in bloom…

How is such productivity possible? Perhaps it's best not to know, and just enjoy the secret sauce. His example proves the maxim that quantity inevitably leads to quality. An exclusive focus on quality paradoxically leads to lower quality work over the grand sweep of time.

We all benefit from his work, whether we pass along a single dollar for his strenuous efforts or not. Swanson pours himself 100% into family and work. His work ethic—artist, family man, neighbor—is unsurpassed. Mystifyingly, he somehow has spare capacity to serve with the rural fire department.

As a writer whose last major work required 74,000 words, I admire his ability to convey an ocean of thought and feeling without a single word.

Upon resolving to become a full-time artist, he committed to painting 10-12 hours per day, and then shopped his body of work around to local galleries. Uncommon focus and determination paved his way.

Only a couple years removed from working for others, he relocated his young family to Duluth's sister city, Växjö, Sweden, for four months. Utterly fascinated, I peppered him with questions for an hour. Speaking less than a year after losing predictable income, I couldn't imagine spending money on anything unessential for basic survival. Adam challenges tightwads like me rather directly.

Swanson scraped out the entire contents of his family's savings to DIY his own artist-in-residence experience on the other side of the world. He knew what he wanted and made it happen, "Damn the torpedoes!" Intentionally placing himself among the unfamiliar—other stints have included Antarctica, residency aboard an ocean research vessel, South Africa, Turkey, and more—dug a deep, drawable well that'll never go dry.

Other than a grant paying his family's airfare to Sweden, expenses were covered through savings and ingenuity. Working through contacts inside the sister cities program, for example, he received a donated studio space within a converted insane asylum now filled with artists. The local joke must be, "What changed?"

They rented a cozy cabin on a lake for $1200 a month, equipped with a wood-fired hot tub (I picture human stew in a large cast-iron pot) and sauna. Friendly landlords proved useful for navigating local culture. The Swansons lived a 30-minute bike ride from the city, and a stellar public transportation system was at their disposal. Sister city leaders donated bus passes and bikes. Life slowed to a simple pace as they fell into a steady rhythm.

Adam, in describing financial nuts and bolts, conveys that it's possible to live outside the usual box. They rented out their Duluth home for the duration, sold a couple paintings in Sweden, gave a bunch a way, and toted 15 pieces home inside his four-year-old's luggage.

Elegant simplicity.

Risk, for those addicted to a paycheck, seems so high. Placed in the balance beside the prospect of lifetime rewards, peril's probability is rendered miniscule.

Returning home penniless, Adam cranked out more paintings to sell. When operating out of abundance, money is a renewable resource. The penny-pincher writing these lines was so inspired that he set up his own writer-in-residence situation at the Food Farm. Though only three days and slightly closer to home, it was no less impactful.

Swanson challenges us to think beyond the limits within which we hem ourselves in, and not to hoard cash. It's taking years for this to sink in, but I'm slowly getting there.

A form of arriving is a growing ability to appreciate such audacity while avoiding the comparison trap. Inspirational seasoning, sans inferiority complex, does brain and body good. 3 days/30 miles vs 4 months/4,000 miles.

Brave and talented creatives are worthy of our time, attention, dollars, and gratitude. Rather than invest energy into far-off elites, do the work of discovering abundant talent in your own backyard. These are people you can actually connect with, who might even return a phone call or email.

Pre-farm, I commented, "I'll more than likely have to get a job at some point…"

Shrugging his shoulders, he replied, "Maybe."

It's what he didn't say, expression speaking volumes, that I found so refreshing. While others take it as a given that alternative lifestyles are all but impossible, creative risk-takers like Adam do not. They're open to possibility. Sitting with such uncommon souls facilitated extraction from a crippling mid-life crisis.
In relaxing, we find buoyancy for escaping quicksand.

I came to Adam's work through my wife, who expressed a desire to collect art for our home. Being a Neanderthal, I found it difficult to part with cash for something "optional" like this. Loving husband that I am, however, we contacted Adam directly to purchase something that had sat around a while for a value price. Pulling up to his little house in a less affluent neighborhood than ours, parked behind their car bearing a bumper sticker saying, "Tree Hugging Dirt Worshipper," the thought, "Toto, we aren't in Kansas anymore," came to mind. Ten minutes later, we shelled out $150 for a large piece, which, after considering a decade of satisfaction, now seems like nothing. Where did the next one fifty go?

To date, this is the only cash we have sent Adam's way. I've enjoyed his work and career across all these years. That's an embarrassingly small price to pay.

The paint's texture itself, heaped onto the board and scraped around liberally, communicates volumes. Content redolent in themes foreshadowing our harrowing journey, deceptively elemental with ample space for interpretation, its value outstripped currency's nominal worth years ago.

Art's immense value eludes the multitudes who embrace mountains of ephemera. Here's Adam's off-the-cuff take on the matter:

I think art is important because it makes people think about stuff. It provides a glimpse of the world through someone else's eyes. It can offer us something contemplative or something energizing. Art definitely has the capacity to inspire people to make changes. Art can make life worth living.

Working as an artist also offers some other things to the world. I am showing my children, and others, that with focus, luck, and hard work, I can spend my days doing something I love. That is a message that's important for anyone to receive. Of course, every person's means and situation is different, but I do believe we can shape our lives no matter what type of situation we are in. Life is full of trades and compromises, but we have to own those and accept them.

22

Ten copies sold out that first weekend, demonstrating the benefits of a monopoly. The Duluth Grill had become renowned for delicious, locally sourced cuisine made from scratch. A single book, "Signed and bike-delivered by Duluth author," placed in front of a captive, buy-local crowd waiting around at all times of day, was like opening a candy stand in front of an elementary school. In contrast to bookstores that stocked two or three at a time, which then moldered around for months among thousands of options, I sold 100 copies here.

Selling at this restaurant, an experiment, trained me to focus on places where my wares stood out. This skill came in handy later on when selecting crops for my urban farm, and helped me react quickly when experiencing the futility of a crowded market that forced a race to the bottom in prices. Rather than spread myself a mile wide and an inch deep, I have dedicated energy into a few niche items placed only where my people shop, rather than all over the place, selling a handful here, there, and everywhere.

This is the 80/20 principle, which posits that 20% of our effort produces 80% of results. Capitalizing on unexpected successes like this—focusing on the most profitable 20%—while cutting out the energy-sapping 80%, similarly enabled my tiniest of farms to succeed against steep odds.

Biking books to the restaurant, in honor of the increasingly annoying sticker touting bike-delivery, required a 20-mile roundtrip. The call to bring more books came at remarkably inconvenient times. Without exception, these excursions became the highlight of my week. Forced exercise intersected with budding friendships, increased connection, curiosity, meaning and purpose, discovery, fresh air, and cherished memories, such as when my ten-year-old joined me for what was then his longest bike ride.

We exchanged all the profits for the most sumptuous breakfast of his life. Afterward, we threw stones into Lake Superior. Joey came within an inch of striking me in the temple with a smooth stone chucked at full strength. Death's door rattled on an idyllic day. Skull performed to safety standards.

Every trip brought renewed perspective and pelted me with desperately needed encouragement.

Deliveries found me ushered into Tom Hanson's office, where he paid invoices immediately. Since he deals with over 100 local vendors—pickle lady arrived during one of our chats—payments are cut on the spot, so an ascent of invoice mountain won't be required later. Though the restaurant was grossing $100k per week, the owner remained approachable and down-to-earth.

He's the exact opposite of most restaurateurs who achieve success and notoriety (appearances on the Food Network, newspaper coverage, etc). Hanson wouldn't last long as CEO of a large corporation. His own profits are an afterthought, almost accidental. He chooses the interesting, sustainable, and community-based.

Tom says, "I prefer to do things the hard way."

It's highly unusual for a restaurant to employ 12 managers, for example, each earning healthy salaries while working reasonable hours. One of these is a farm manager, who oversees an ambitious urban farm. My experience with employers was that they continually heaped more work on employees, increasing stress and turnover, while keeping a bit more of the profits for themselves with every turn of the ratchet. The Duluth Grill is the exact opposite.

The breath of fresh air is palpable. Fulfilled workers are proud to work there: from dishwasher to owner. I greeted employees across the hierarchy during a busy lunch. Everyone, even the dishwasher, produced an immense smile. Here they are part of a movement, and not a bottom line.

Tom treated me to a full kitchen tour. His son, quietly engaged in food prep, brought to mind another restaurant owner's heir. Whenever Daddy wasn't around, he stomped around his fiefdom all puffed up on delusional self-importance, causing earnest workers to scurry off like cockroaches.

Like a magician eager to show off his latest trick, Hanson conveyed me to the cooler, where rabbit meat marinated in some mystical concoction for 24 hours. The bunnies were raised on veggie scraps collected from restaurant and gardens. Rabbits reproduce so rapidly that a single pair can produce 50% more meat annually than a year-old beef steer. Farm-to-table sustainability grows to new heights as Hanson and Co continually push boundaries outward.

Skeptically, we returned to the Grill on a rare date night. Rabbit meat was tender and delectable, a marvelous experience, particularly after visiting the inspiring urban oasis that produced it.

Meanwhile, Tom could live high off the hog, drunk on accolades showered upon him by the media and community. He has remained in the same modest home for decades, in the gritty part of town where his life's work has concentrated.

His neighbors must have been incredulous when he blasted apart his driveway to create more growing space and a flower-lined walking path leading to lavish gardens. Entering his backyard is a feast for the senses, causing me to consider greater possibilities for my own similarly-sized space. Entering this alternate reality was enthralling, a place of unimaginable bounty within an average city lot.

Employing a farm manager, gardener, and a botanist, the financial impact is considerable. Ambitious restaurateurs typically call it one and done with a distributor or two. Hanson's approach is an all-consuming lifestyle. The eruption of beauty overflows and rubs off on the community. Will such extravagances that have infused character into the restaurant's culture survive the chaos wrought by COVID 19? This profile is a snapshot in time.

Possessing more dreams than space, Tom had just purchased the neighboring home. A winding switchback path was being built into steep terrain. Accommodating a valued wheelchair-bound botanist required intense effort and design.

Devotion.

Hanson ensures his people are happy, challenged, and fulfilled. Indulging farm manager Francois Medion's wild ideas must not have been cheap. Examples include the massive space-consuming hugelkultur garden in the restaurant's always filled parking lot, or the 25-foot-long aquaponics system inside the greenhouse in Tom's backyard, which he hoped to fill with hundreds of pacu fish for the menu. I don't believe that experiment panned out, a victim of our frigid winter.

The Grill's culture encourages wild risk-taking that keeps the best employees engaged and loyal. Major financial outlays seem to ignore standard return on investment calculations.

Francois must have been among the planet's most fortunate farmers. The man is an artist, and definitely not a businessman. I felt rapturous joy for his good fortune in finding the perfect niche. He bursts with utopian ideas that those chained to colorless practicality ridicule. Having come of age in France, the guy literally worked in the circus. His conception of reality and how we might improve things is further to the left. Congenial, radical voices like his are incredibly valuable amidst community conversation. People like Francois help us think beyond, adding an otherwise unattainable richness.

Hanson's journey might one day consume a book. Eschewing college education for the school of hard knocks, his debts kept the restaurant in a tenuous state for years. A last minute loan from a waitress kept a mortgage from falling through at a dire moment, and credit card loans lubricated payroll. As with others in this quest, decades of perseverance and grit built the empire.

I took in far more from these fascinating people than I ever gave back in tangible value through newspaper columns and blog posts. They generously opened lives to me simply because I was curious and took time to venture down the rabbit hole.

None of these encounters directly forged me into someone capable of adding value to the community, or paid commensurately. Far more significant, they challenged patterns of thinking that held me back. Ruts are not easily abandoned. Their very presence is often so subtle that you can't quite put your finger on them. Artists, farmers, and entrepreneurs build their lives through alternative thinking, being, and, most importantly, DOING.

23

As quarter-life and midlife crises merged like unruly eyebrows, I endlessly asked, "What should I do with my life?"

Analysis paralysis created a logjam impossible to think myself out of. Liberation from those La Brea Tar Pits brought spectacular clarity: just do. The only thing that changed was I had nothing to lose. I simply did things that interested me.

Liberated from a taskmaster's direction, an ideal day contained three parts: brains, brawn, and commerce. Fulfillment requires mental challenge, using our noodle at capacity to grab hold of ideas and tasks just outside our usual grasp. Physical body demanded a similar level of engagement with the world as my brain. Engaging in commerce by providing value to my neighbors in some small way (selling, working, trading, serving, whatever) was also critical.

All three were impossible inside a comfortable cubicle, where brain and body developed kindred flabbiness. Like a gorilla in a small enclosure, isolation walled me off from participating in the dynamic local economy that you can feel, smell, taste, hear, and see.

The pursuit began rather humbly. All I had was a master's degree in a subject given short shrift, an ability to wield a bit of humor, and some willingness to scrape off flakes of paint and reapply it. Slate wiped clean, I started over from the bottom rung.

Ignorance's depth knows no bounds, facilitating lifelong adventure and discovery. To loosely quote Epictetus, "You can't learn what you think you already know." There's so very much to delight in, ponder, and work out. Those poor souls who seem to have everything figured out are missing the marrow.

When opportunity knocked, I took on a part-time, minimum wage job at the Food Farm. A lifelong dream, I fantasized about having the words BONAFIDE FARMER emblazoned onto a belt buckle.

What would minimum wage feel like? Our family's few purchases became imbued with a value that's difficult to understand without experiencing for yourself. To illustrate, here's a portion of a review I wrote for Mayor Ness's book, Hillsider:

This book is worth every penny. The purchase required nearly half a day's wage of me, since I am currently laboring as a farmhand at minimum wage. I couldn't be more pleased. The book is even more valuable than the sweat exchanged for it while toiling under the sun.

"More valuable than the sweat exchanged for it," became criteria for all purchases.

Rather than hide reality from our children, we shared the burden within a context of gratitude. The most unexpected moments pierced our hearts, such as when my daughter asked me to retrieve her brush after a long day. She was in the midst of a summer on crutches, lumbering around with a cumbersome cast, unable to swim. Her face radiated pride as she said, "That's my brush…" There was so much in that look. Happiness. Contentment. Love. Shawna shelled out three bucks for the nine-year-old to have her own brush.

Emma's countenance beamed with gratitude, still touched some days later. This simple moment, impossible to manufacture, filled me with joy as we learned to navigate a lifestyle with far less cash. Gifts shrank in size and frequency.

Pecuniary scarcity blessed our kids, but it was stressful. They learned we couldn't afford many "things," and grappled with my refusal to attach adjectives like "poor" to the situation. Possessions, though few, were held in trust. They were to be loved. Cared for. Honored. Nothing was taken for granted: utilitarian objects like the brush, clean running water pouring from a tap, or chickens pumping out fresh eggs.

One morning cupboards were bereft of breakfast food. Nesting boxes had produced no eggs, but Shawna sent our son to check one more time.

He raced back to the house, overjoyed. She'd have just enough to whip up delicious pancakes. Luckily, in his excitement, he didn't drop them! This miraculous provision stamped itself indelibly upon his formation.

Household economy required pulling together.

A day of oppressive heat and humidity found me happily at home on a day off. Luxuriously, I considered my hard-working compatriots moving down the rows beneath a scorching sun as I finished the last 150 pages of The Grapes of Wrath, guilt-free in an air-conditioned room.

The book was a novel experience while laboring at $58/day, security's thin veneer smashed. Though published in 1939, such hardship is generationally adjacent. My grandfather was 29 years old at the time.

Desperate migrant workers perform back-breaking work without benefit of minimum wage. Due to mass migration out of the Dust Bowl, labor's supply exceeded demand. Children died of starvation. A day's work failed to feed a family. The story—conjoined with my work at the farm—was a vivid reminder that Jesus is on the side of the poor.

Steinbeck excoriates power's abuse and wealth's concentration, a theme for the ages. Judgmental church-goers, blind to God's hostility toward injustice, express tremendous consternation at trivialities like dancing, but remain willfully silent about an unfolding human tragedy. For probably the first time, I felt the enormous value in feeling angry about those things that provoke God.

The most profound realizations are correspondingly simple.

Connections happen organically by joining brains, brawn, and meaningful commerce. A dash of soul infused to the trio renders magic.

The day I arrived ten minutes late following a 138-minute commute through a persistent headwind stands out. I pedaled directly to the field without taking a break, feeling like I was transitioning between stages of a triathlon.

After abandoning my career's furthering, expectant hope relocated itself into the present, where I became fully enmeshed, aware of everyday beauty and the smallest coincidences, generating a state of perpetual awe. The Quest, though intensely physical, was equally spiritual.

En route, I had infiltrated a large corporate function that later featured Cheryl Strayed, the famous author, as keynote speaker. Serendipitously, my bright green shirt was an exact match to the gleaming t-shirts sported by hundreds of employees milling around outside the venue. It felt like I was supposed to be there, attempting an act of guerrilla-marketing for the ages. After fording through the great throng of humanity in search of the organization's mole, and being steered by a well-placed friend, "He's one of the purple shirts," I placed a copy of my book into the hands of the man who later gave it to Cheryl. I suppose she "forgot" it in the back of the limo, but no matter. Accomplishing something so audacious was exhilarating.

Hours later, in loam so soft and rich I couldn't resist working barefoot, I pulled an agate. Then, at the moment I looked up, I discovered my fellow farmhand wore the same shirt I had recently donated to a thrift store. Broken button was unmistakable. What are the odds? What does this mean??? Surely significant!

A photo captures her beautiful, smiling face as I relayed stupefaction.

Cynicism and guile—pigeon excrement concealing sculpture's beauty—washed away. Childlike naïveté and wonder bloomed unabashed. The only fella kneeling in the dirt alongside 20-something females, middle-aged and marooned, I was mysteriously joyful and content.

In that same photo, beside the gal who now leads the farm crew, you'll discover 40 five-gallon buckets filled with the best carrots money can buy. I dumped them all, and another load just like it, into the carrot-washer. Irrational joy in performing the task made me chuckle at being a bit like Louis Anderson (similar age and career prospects) in the movie, Coming to America:

I started out harvesting leeks, and moved on to cabbages. Now I'm washing carrots and potatoes. Soon I'll be driving the tractor!

Later, it was thrilling to pack these carrots and potatoes for delivery to the Duluth Grill, which I visited a handful of days earlier to gather grist for a newspaper column. There's nothing quite like plumbing obsession's depths for spurring life change.

With a bright light affixed to handlebars illuminating the last several miles, I returned home to my other job as the family's dishwasher. The 12-hour day was exhausting, and I was dirty. Honest, wholesome work felt amazing.

Our young flock of chickens began laying eggs on that very day, weeks earlier than expected, at just 20 weeks of age. Once again, what does it mean???? (Cheryl Strayed, agate, shirt, carrots, 60 miles biked on the fall equinox, all on the same day.) Everything takes on deep spiritual meaning in such moments. We became grateful for God's provision, through the humble chicken, of high-protein eggs every day.

When you put yourself out there, and I mean way out to the point of being unsure of what you're doing, having released any claim to the future while letting go of financial anxiety and resting in simple faith that you and yours will be cared for, small miraculous moments are like jet fuel.

I continued pushing my book into the world, a slog of moving individual copies, but I also attended events to expand my limited reach. Setting up shop alongside more traditional vendors at the Lester River Rendezvous, I had a slight advantage in selling the only book.

I was proud of the display that featured several items from my story. The bright red union suit on a clothesline was a nod to airing out dirty laundry. Nobody asked about that. I sat in a chair, placed an extra beside me, and invited free conversations. The goal was to provide an oasis while unloading ten books.

The first two hours were an existential struggle. A dour fellow stopped by after spying Perfect Duluth Day's glowing review pasted to the table, which also featured Mayor Ness's book. He ranted for ten minutes about Don's parking policies, like Merlin summoning a curse. The Mayor was leaving office at the apex of his career. I hadn't realized that someone with a Fidel Castro-like 89% approval rating faced such intense enemies.

Regardless of political differences, it's helpful to remember that these are people with families, not enemies in opposing foxholes.

Negativity seeped into my patch of real estate like an oil spill, repelling all customers. Two hours in, I had yet to sell a single copy or make a connection. How easy it is to fall into depression at these times! This, after all the work required to set up, and sacrificing a Saturday with my wife and kids. Adding insult to injury, I harvested cabbages like a migrant worker the day before. What was I doing with my life?

At this lowest point, clouds literally parted as a beam of sunlight cut through the foggy mist and an angel visited my booth. She didn't purchase a book, but the woman was so positive, warm, and supportive, it didn't matter. The stopper pulled from the bathtub. Negativity drained away.

Selling 11 books required all the perseverance and grit I could muster. A single book on an attractive table isn't enough to make a living. This was worth enduring, if only for the sake of understanding how market booths attract interest.

Back to the fields I went, realizing that events were an inefficient use of time. I helped bring in all the late season crops: cabbage, carrots, potatoes, rutabagas, winter squash, etc. Kneeling in cold soil beside a dedicated crew racing to collect the last of the potatoes after sunset as a stiff northerly wind bears down with threat of rain, kindles camaraderie.

Married with children, there was none of the former tension that previously existed in close company among young females. With so much life ahead of them, and few responsibilities nailing them down, it was marvelous to hear of their hopes and dreams. None of us had cell phones playing podcasts or music in our ears. We entertained each other with stories and questions. Our many differences—life experience, politics, worldview, biological makeup—mattered not. In fact, it was their very differentness that made them fascinating. Their wholesomeness was perhaps most surprising of all.

Clad in coveralls, our future crew leader glows with earthy, natural beauty. She met her husband at a folk dance, of all things, and possesses no aspirations for wealth. Her ambitions included, "A little house, a patch of raspberries, and a couple kids."

The friendly, engaging gal on her left (cabbage-picking buddies in the beautiful photo taken out on the Back 40) was learning fiddle-style on her violin. Rather than sitting around watching movies or mindlessly consuming entertainment created with no sense of place, she and her roommates played small Americana concerts in an adjacent field. Front porch jam sessions were as ubiquitous as in early 20th century Appalachia.

Praiseworthy aspects of their lifestyle—perhaps even more analog than their grandparents—abound. Our basic desires to love and be loved are remarkably analogous. Entire elements of our population, both left and right, wall themselves off in cultural enclaves and miss out on these surprising discoveries. Rather than readying arrows for that next sortie in an unending culture war, I opted out.

I came to love these people, almost by accident, by kneeling in the soil beside them while engaged in basic tasks necessary for human survival. Simple, childlike apprehension of beauty in those who have radically different perspectives on life could bring healing to our fractured land. This antidote to a pluralistic society pulling itself apart at the seams is free and available to all.

24

Attempting to get ahead of a flurry of interview requests, I emailed Emily Larson a week before the mayoral election:

Brace yourself for what may be the weirdest request you'll receive today.

I'm a local author. I've been hankering to invite myself over for dinner, literally. LOL, I know how strange that sounds. However, I think a "down home" atmosphere will make for a splendid conversation with you and the family, and a very cool column or blog post in the end. Plus, I'd just like to get to know you...
Is there any chance I could stop by for dinner some time after the election? I'd love to help with meal prep, dishes, and the whole thing. Regardless of the outcome, I wish to pursue this. Yes, it's weird, but undeniably awesome. Not only am I wishing to do a blog post and possibly a newspaper column (we'll see, and

there's no bloody pressure to perform at all—in fact, that would ruin the experience), but I'm also writing a book in praise of local. Politics, and the beauty of being able to rub shoulders with local leaders, will play a small role in the book. I look forward to including meaningful experiences like this in the finished product. Basically, I'm smitten by local food, visual artists, political leaders, musicians, neighbors, community, and wish to share this with others...

Choosing to guard her family's private life, Larson declined my generous offer of helping with the dishes, but agreed to connect after the election. Arriving at her modest home, my assumptions rose to the surface and withered away. Exuding warmth and authenticity, she was neither wealthy, aloof, nor unapproachable. In contradistinction to the cold-blooded reptile expected, I was greeted by a normal human being with a regular, relatable family life.

Once inside, I admired the large painting hanging beside a bank of 100-year-old windows and woodwork. A strong piece, the penguins, bike, and hot air balloons are vintage Adam Swanson. The photograph I snapped of Emily standing before it evokes the magic swirling about our community. There is real power that comes with immersing ourselves in the God-given talent of those around us that is qualitatively different than something pretty, but generic, from the big box store.

Neither Swanson nor Larson were born in Duluth. They're both transplants, as am I, but are as enmeshed into the community's story as one can be, which is what I sought, and seek. Notoriety isn't the goal, mind you, but a sense of my family's cog integrating into body politic's machinery.

Another smile in my collection, snapshot conveys Emily's enhanced vigor through connection, fine-tuned to Duluth's strengths and weaknesses. Visual art and politics, callings as distinct as east and west, overlap. Right here, at the intersection of seemingly unrelated gifts, sparks fly. Just as his work isn't merely the application of paint to panel, or hers the oversight of road maintenance, art happens when empathy or deeply felt need ricochets within a person's DNA and life experiences, and overflows into a peculiar means of expression.

Similar to the Mayor choosing what was, for her taste, the very best painting Adam had made available to the world, we all may delight in the choicest cut of beef, jewel in the crown, or pick of the bunch. Rather than hamstringing our own happiness and ability to connect with others through a false sense of righteous indignation over political differences or lifestyle choices, we might simply enjoy the great art erupting all around us. Be it potatoes, paintings, political skill in forging relationships, or prose, a childlike ability to delight in these offerings is perhaps the easiest (and most enjoyable) means of binding up a rapidly disintegrating society.

⚜

After swaddling ourselves in winter coats, hats, and gloves, we stepped into the season's first frigid blast. Fall had been long and merciful until this moment of freeze-up. Emily's breathtaking view across Lake and City seemed fitting for a helmsman. She exuded gratitude for a gorgeous, crisp morning, never complaining about the temperature (12 degrees, down from a recent 60) or ice, betraying her outdoorsy mettle.

Effortless navigation of steep, slippery terrain in trail-running shoes became a point of connection. Trail runners spot one another as easily as accountants geeking out over spreadsheets. In any meeting of human beings, contrary worldviews and assumptions notwithstanding, some commonality presents itself as a foothold. Patience and careful observation are the only requisites.

At last, our meandering journey brought us to the Snooty Fox, where we enjoyed, "Tea for Two." Some years have passed since this conversation (she's now finishing her second term), but I remain smitten, proving out something she said. "Everybody has a story. If you just slow down and listen to it, you can find yourself in that story. Once you've slowed down and connected with that story, you can't undo that. You'll have a loyalty to that story forever."

Emily succinctly rattled off several specifics that caused her to connect with my story. Arrows struck my heart, bypassing the brain, so I cannot recall them. Those few minutes of complete vulnerability were so encouraging, questioning my role in society as I was, and being, "One of the least of these..."

Sitting across the table from her, at a loss for words while gazing out the window, I relayed the story about the crank who despised Ness over some parking differences, and left a cloud of negativity over my Rendezvous booth. His full-throated hatred conveyed the sheer antagonistic force besetting the most popular mayor in our history. Emily confirmed that 89% approval rating often means intense hatred from the remaining 11%.

I might disagree with Larson 60% of the time, but remain grateful for her service. In bonding with her on a personal level, I discovered an exceptional human being. She carved out two hours in granting me her first interview as Mayor-elect, putting off a long list of requests that included national publications. Emily radiates warmth and authenticity, genuinely desiring success for people like me: strugglers.

The health of a community is on display in its attitude toward elected leaders. Citizens are proud to live here, blessed as we are by abundant natural beauty and resources, an usually strong cadre of artists, a resurgent craft movement (from beer to backpacks), and a renewed love for all things local. There is a more robust sense of place here than any other I've encountered (something like Fenway Park, but without the irrational Yankee-hatred).

Thus, we feel offended when trolls make disparaging remarks of our Mayor, as well we should. This doesn't mean we should agree with 100% of the Mayor's agenda, or even vote for them. Rather, we have a subconscious sense that she represents the very best of us as a community. A healthy, fulfilled citizenry has grace for their leaders. We love them despite their flaws, simultaneously enjoying their relatable humanity. We're grateful for their many sacrifices.

The most valuable thing you may offer your community is friendship. Be a good neighbor. Citizenship involves more than voting. It seems many of us have forgotten this most basic concept. It's difficult to hate someone you care for, or, dare I say it, love.

The vast majority of their efforts are apolitical meat and potato issues: fixing streets, maintaining parks, fire department budgets, and other matters so boring that we barely give a moment's thought. These necessaries aren't laying groundwork for turning over sovereignty to the United Nations. When we disagree on the occasional hot-button issue, it's helpful to remember that a snap judgment often arises from spending five minutes in a short news story. She may have devoted 100 hours to struggling over the same conundrum in coming to an imperfect course of action, agreeing to compromises along the way.

By virtue of a single conversation, I've enjoyed eight years of strong affinity for my Mayor. Might this be a more pleasant existence than nearly a decade of antipathy, distrust, and soul-eroding malice? The cost of connection is low, but the payout is high.

25

After Mayor Ness casually said, "We should do a book event together," I mulled over possibilities for weeks. My book events distinguished themselves as forays into purgatory. Time stopped. Boredom reigned supreme.

How might we escape monotony?

While ruminating on six months of tectonic upheaval since my book's release, a cornucopia sprang to mind. I was gathering friendships, becoming acquainted with artists, farmers, entrepreneurs, and community leaders. With much of prior existence confined to a hole in the ground, I was stunned to uncover so much richness by tapping into the incredible energy of our talent-laden community.

All this beauty—humanity in bloom—previously escaped my notice. Life became oriented around reaping the local harvest and sharing it with others. This was a time for thanksgiving: for outgoing Mayor's service, the burgeoning community of artists, and local producers of every shape, shade, and variety.

In stark contrast to authors confined behind a table, potential bottled up, this would be a feast for the senses. My goal, rather than book sales, was to foster a bonanza of local goodness that might ignite a passion for integrating the giftedness of neighbors into all aspects of life.

With local talent as a unifying theme, the notion of a variety show materialized. Jobless, moving around by bike while groping for my place, I discovered the relative ease of reorienting life around the community through immersion.

Charlie Parr committed to playing the event early on, so I had two huge names to leverage for scoring a venue and attracting more acts. The task was all-consuming for two months, challenging me in new and exciting ways. This big lift showed I could accomplish great things if I only pushed forward in following the breadcrumbs, turning over one stone at a time. Also noteworthy: I had no budget.

With "America's most popular mayor" (a national headline) on my side, and Charlie Parr, a local musician with a rabid following, I found courage for approaching the most desirable showcase: The Red Herring Lounge. A downtown hotspot, it was the hippest joint around. Similar to my eventual practice of building farm customers by entering chef's kitchen with luscious tray of pea shoots on my arm like it was a supermodel, I approached enigmatic proprietor, Bob Monahan, with the idea.

Arriving at the establishment atop my 25-year-old bicycle, it was marvelous to greet somebody so completely and wildly other: trendy bachelor vs plain middle-aged dad, stylish hair vs thinning locks, "out there" liberal vs former seminary student, urban hipster vs budding man of the soil. Amazingly, we hit it off. Bob loved the idea from the get-go, and booked a free night posing scant risk of lost business: Tuesday before Thanksgiving. Not only was the facility a natural fit, catering to concert-goers nightly, it alleviated any need to provide refreshments or expend precious energy on the many details that come with hosting hundreds of people.

With wind in my sails, I approached Trampled By Turtles. At the height of the band's stardom, appearing on such stages as Late Night with David Letterman, they mercifully declined. It was the only, "No thanks, but best of luck," reinforcing my conviction to never shy away from asking. In my experience, people rarely say no. When they do, it mysteriously reinforces overall success. TBT would have overshadowed everyone else.

Local brewers, authors, top-notch musicians (Tin Can Gin, Teague Alexy, and Dave Hundrieser joined the lineup), visual artists, a tap dancer, and not one but two mayors (incoming and outgoing), all responded with a resounding, "Yes!"

While handling publicity myself, I found an odd thrill in putting my master's degree to practical use. The physical object rested within a large, unwieldy folder perfect for toting around oversized promotional posters. Biking to two dozen locations, I pulled the formerly useless folder (pomp and circumstance) from my backpack to unveil a fancy degree in juxtaposition to the posters. At every stop, understanding grew of a palpable relationship between theology and the creative output of neighbors.

Loving God and loving neighbor, created in the very image thereof, reinforces one another. Is genuine love even possible without uncovering and enjoying those peculiar heaven-sent qualities manifesting as talent? This simple observation became a passion.

Obsession, actually.

Rather than struggling to understand how I might serve my neighbor in more traditional ways, I uncovered immense joy by delighting in their unique genius, always sensing greater benefit from them than they from me. Realization that loving and serving others needn't be expensive or complicated was liberating.

Low circumstances became a catalyst for understanding and feeling this truth deep down in my core. Our particular aptitude, when allowed to flower into overflow as an offering for society, pushes outward to the furthest reaches of one's blast radius. Just as I'm doing right now in this book, humans genuinely want others to see and savor what they have discovered, thus offering entry into their circle. Abundant opportunity exists to bask in this radiant brilliance. Elevating your neighbors while pointing out and sharing their giftedness with others, overlooking flaws, is service.

This book has been an eight-year struggle. Can you imagine the heartbreak if my offering is ignored? This work is akin to discovering fire and carrying coals back to society. Each of us, bearing embers, similarly long for others to discern their potential use and beauty. Delight.

Most folks I approached for this event, and also in my travels throughout the community, seemed more talented and generous than me. Starting over from scratch, I had little to offer of tangible value.

Intangibles—friendship, respect, admiration—are of greater import.

Complete liberation from posturing, or appearing worthy of respect, was remarkable. Paradoxically, this low station in life garnered more regard, esteem, and connection (even from my own children) than my previously "respectable" state of affairs.

Our unvarnished selves more clearly display the divine spark. People admire this simple beauty. This realization, something I never could have predicted or intuited without experiencing, provided courage for approaching anyone along the entire spectrum of success. Upon encountering an open person with the drawbridge down, virtually all mortals lower their guard as well, becoming more willing to help.

I joked I'd bolt out the door by 10 pm so my transformation back to village idiot wouldn't occur in public, but there were more legitimate concerns. As Herculean as these efforts were, no income rolled into coffers. Making matters worse, nothing was planned for after clock struck midnight. I knew the mother of all depressions was waiting. Nothing could stop it. Accepting reality, I chose to enjoy the ride.

26

Hosting Cornucopia was like running with wild horses.

A favorite snapshot captures the evening's spirit. Pearly white teeth and rosy red cheeks testify to pure, unvarnished joy.

Outgoing Mayor is leaving office at the top of his game. Teacher beside him has soldiered on for decades. Is one more important than the other?

A month earlier, I crossed a high school threshold for the first time since fleeing mine. The educator radiates ebullience and genuine passion for her subject and students, who adore her. Seeing her in action was like witnessing an endangered species accomplishing some vital purpose within its ideal habitat. The visit—delivering a stack of my books for potential class discussion—filled me with hope for the high school experience awaiting my children.

As luck would have it, my daughter is ensconced in her class right now. By all appearances, this teacher's enthusiasm and zest have only increased with time.

Does she have flaws? You bet. Perhaps she's a raging alcoholic. Seems unlikely. By not dwelling on others' defects, we may reap a harvest from our neighbors' finest offerings. Nearly everyone has a one-of-a-kind gifting, best enjoyed through simple childlike wonder.

My pair of rose-colored glasses filters out blemishes and enhances beauty. Go get yo self a pair.

Marinading in the talents of neighbors—unbridled gratitude expressed through enjoyment—enriches all.

The Mayor and teacher are equally valuable and necessary. In the image, she's excited to get a copy of Hillsider directly from his hand. As with all the books I saw him sign and personalize, Don made the purchaser feel special. He mentioned meeting her 11 years earlier at the Homegrown Music Festival. The photo depicts the accessibility of supposed "celebrities" in our community, and probably yours. My goal was for everyone to experience this reality, feeling in their very bones that there are no little people.

Talents—shared, appreciated, overlapping, and stacked— rain blessings down on all. Unforeseen connections occurring within intersections of our peculiar talents are magical.

Red Herring Lounge filled to capacity on a normally dead evening. Successful beyond my wildest expectations, people of all ages and walks of life exuded unrestrained joy. Even Patty, a no-nonsense woman who serves at my hardware store with six decades of life experience behind her, found it enjoyable. With so few seats available, I asked if she gouged somebody's eyes out to land a barstool. Numerous non-hipster types similarly partook.

Mayor-elect Emily Larson delivered a generous toast to kick the evening off, thanking Ness for his years of service. Both she and Ness were non-political in their remarks, holding the crowd transfixed.

All the performers similarly carried the water effortlessly.

In contrast, as the evening's host, I intended to speechify, but found myself tongue-tied. Thankfully, no lofty language was required. At one point I picked up my book for a full eight minutes, a character-building experience if there ever was one. Energized crowd wanted more music, NOT a reading. Later, in the green room, a 20-something gal greeted me in all sincerity, saying, "I enjoyed your poetry tonight."

#notapoet

Donny read a page from his book—a short, amusing tale with a beginning, middle, and end, punctuated by a hilarious photograph—spellbinding all. Holding a crowd's attention is an art form.

Rabbit hole descended ever onward, as I immersed all aspects of life more fully into the community. Though our family's income placed us well below the poverty line, life increasingly revolved around our locality. Developing a sense of place while sinking down roots is Adventure.

This just might have been the finest community event of 2015. It's mystifying that an unemployed, broken down writer without a budget could pull it off and attract such luminaries.

If I could make these connections over the course of six months on a peasant's income, and find such meaning and fulfillment in doing so, you can too. In fact, you can do it better and more easily than me. Delight in nearby bounty: beauty in the landscape and people, visual arts, literary works, food and drinks, and offerings from more makers than you can imagine. We all benefit when even one additional family enmeshes themselves into the immediate economy.

Far too many people, in a misguided notion of saving money, are bereft of knowledge or understanding of local producers. This reverberates into permanent disconnection from neighbors.

How can we love our neighbor, or even fulfill our purpose in life, if we willfully ignore their contribution to society?

While telecommuting from a cold basement, I welcomed the company of spiders in lieu of genuine camaraderie. Toiling away in those deep, dark bowels of Corporate America, I was a polyp. The painful act of being snipped off granted freedom for embedding into the community instead.

Immense talent exists in people all around us. Let us fix our attention on them, rather than far-off celebrities who don't share common values or care about much, if anything, beyond themselves. We need not look toward distant lands at a drab monoculture, both withered and bloated by its own excesses, for our cues. A feast is set all around you. Partake.

Act III

Never let a good depression go to waste.

27

As predicted, the deepest depression of my life commenced the morning after. Though the event was a triumph, I was no closer to charting out a future.

I was a kind of mini-celebrity. Thousands of readers enjoyed my newspaper column and website, finding inspiration in the unusual approach to midlife crisis navigation. Book sales relentlessly continued their downward trend, however. Achieving notoriety or fame wasn't the path forward. Now what?

Melancholy is beneficial in the long run. In darkness, we grope for any faint flicker of light. Small things, otherwise overlooked, arise within our altered perspective, begetting a sweetness and beauty impossible to appreciate when life is humming along on all cylinders. These tiny flares, invisible under the brightness of day, are beacons in the darkness. Hope, mysterious and elusive, unfurls in unexpected places.

My rehab program revolved around establishing

meaningful connections with, and within, the community. This included working the soil, biking Duluth's length and breadth while coming to appreciate its nooks and crannies, becoming acquainted with nearby farmers, and partaking in the land's fruitfulness. I enjoyed lengthy conversations with remarkable people who earned a living by employing innate talents that contributed to society. Hours of immersion—steeping—with political leaders, men and women of the soil, bakers, shopkeepers, artists, artisans, tradespeople, mothers and fathers, piled up into weeks and months. An array of individual ingredients, these, some assembly was required.

Feeling useless and feeble, I stumbled upon a recipe for breakfast casserole. Though I rarely cook, this was one of those brief flashes of light. Looking ahead to Saturday morning with eagerness, I gathered the constituent parts.

Having grown the potatoes and eggs myself, I had a head start. Hunting down the very best sausage, local bacon, and other sundries became that week's mission. This gathering was a quest for synergy, wherein the combined effect is greater than the sum of its parts. Expectant hope grew and grew, of far greater value than the finished product.

When the big day arrived, I raced down the stairs like a kid on Christmas morning. The individual tasks were simple, but it took me longer to produce that casserole than it takes some people to run 26.2 miles.

It turned out well enough, and my kids put on an admirable display of enjoying second breakfast. They sensed the pan contained far more than eggs, hash browns, butter, sausage, and bacon. It was the offspring of hope, held together by the fruit of the land.

Eighteen months after the great severing, I remained aimless; cast adrift upon a sea of hopelessness. Establishing mooring in turbulence—a niche within a growing sense of place—can't be ramrodded into reality. It required plumbing the depths of rabbit holes, which, by themselves, seemed nonsensical. Bound together within the overall pilgrimage, however, they were essential for becoming something other than what I had been.

A lifetime spent studying for the test, of assigning numerical values to everything, has a way of reducing meaning to the transactional. If I put this much in, I should get this much out. Return on investment has a place, but it's an inappropriate guidepost at this stage of the journey.

Opening myself to brief flashes of light required shedding a tendency to over-analyze and quantify. Waiting patiently for any small flicker of insight, and then acting upon it, proved invaluable.

Amidst all that darkness, I could hardly see beyond my own two feet.

With very little going on, I rushed to the mailbox in pajamas at 9:30 am every day, seconds after it arrived. Reaching outside, I'd glance leftward and catch my elderly neighbor in her nightgown doing the same. "This is what I've become. At 39..." Working neighbors—bonafide professionals—had long since hustled off to jobs serving a real purpose.

The street was empty, bereft of parked cars. A ghost town.

At peak bewilderment, the Whole Food Co-op's quarterly publication arrived in our mailbox. In a desperate search for some spark of interest, I turned to an inspiring story of a 16-year-old urban farmer's garlic enterprise. A photo featured the boy-proprietor in a shirt bearing a simple message:

Grow food. Ride bike.

The imperative called out so strongly that I launched off the couch, via cannon, to purchase this special garlic for planting, though we were on the cusp of winter. An absurdly mild December day, the clouds had descended to ground level. Dreariness was complete and total. A week of rain and minimal visibility, brought on by El Niño, mirrored my soul. Perhaps I should have pounded the pavement in search of work, but this felt like a foothold for climbing out of the abyss.

Arriving at the Co-op, breathless and wild-eyed with jacket zipped over pajamas, I was crestfallen to learn they were sold out of the hyperlocal garlic that shook me out of a stupor. The produce manager, Nick, climbed up from the store's bowels to cheerfully assist a despairing customer, engaging in a deep-dive of Portlandia-type questions about where the bulk garlic came from, varietal options, fitness for the northland, and then some. Amazingly, he later became my point of entry as a producer myself.

Success in December seemed so improbable that I tracked down Food Farm's right hand man for advice. His few words of encouragement were essential for following through with this most basic of tasks. How did I transform from this lack of courage and understanding to starting my own urban farm in just five months?

In desperation, I submerged 14 individual cloves of garlic into cold, saturated dirt in the midst of an icy rain. Pulling back a layer of rotting leaves to reveal my canvas, I came upon what Aristotle describes as, "The intestines of the earth," an earthworm, wriggling and writhing like a sea serpent brought up from the deep. Life!

Kneeling as a supplicant at the very bottom of a midlife crisis, I planted hope.

The cloves, each containing the mystery and potential of new life, were like Jack's magic beans. As the rain continued pounding for several more days, I wondered if tiny roots were emerging. It wasn't much, but it helped carry me through. At roughly the same moment those tender green shoots emerged in the spring of 2016, I knew what I wanted to do with my life.

It wasn't just the garlic, of course, but that mysterious synergy of faith, hope, love, mystery, wonder, and action coalescing into magic. For this to happen, one must be fully present in the bleakness. You can't wish circumstances away. Feel them, acknowledge reality, and slowly move forward into the unknown.

28

My quest for local garlic stymied, I reached out to the family instead. Rabbit hole, deep and beguiling, sucked me in.

The Fierek family live on the harbor side of Minnesota Point. Gorgeous in any direction, they're situated between great bodies of water, facing an oceangoing sea harbor further inland than any other on the planet. Atop one of the largest freshwater sandbars to be found, this is the demarcation between Lake Superior and the St. Louis River estuary.

Two boys, 16 and 12, operated separate entrepreneurial enterprises tied to the land and water sustaining them. Just seven miles upstream, in a previous era, was the genesis of all this abundance.

Their father, Robert, grew up in the Morgan Park neighborhood, a US Steel company town. His grandfather worked at the steel mill for 44 years, and his dad put in 33. Young Bob would surely continue the tradition. The massive operation was the height of industrialization in these parts. Local shipyards, employing 6,000 people during World War II, used steel from the mill to produce 230 warships. U.S. Steel, forged by the legendary J.P. Morgan, seemed as permanent as bedrock. Until it wasn't…

Strong, burly men wept in public when the mill's closure was announced. Bob recalls a skilled worker looking straight up into the air for answers with tears in his eyes. With just a few years remaining before he could collect a pension, he'd be reduced to pushing a broom after relocating his family to Gary, Indiana. As much of Morgan Park packed up to leave, Bob realized that a big company couldn't be relied upon for one's sole livelihood. The occasion steeled him into carving out a living by his own wits and sweat.

While working as a carpenter, he saw tools sold by people in suits who were unaware of the evolving landscape of equipment and building techniques. Storage options were based on dated concepts, like tool belts for hammers and nails. Nail guns were new to the scene. Carpenters laid these expensive tools on the ground with no place to put them.

He invented the Bucket Boss tool storage system as a solution, which is a canvas apron strapped to a five-gallon bucket. Simple. Inexpensive. Easily reproduced.

From there, an array of items were developed and marketed through a company called Portable Products, which began as a simple eight-page catalog. He and his brother parlayed growing expertise into the formation of Duluth Trading Company, specializing in workwear designed and tested by tradesmen. The company thrived through original design, such as the Longtail T-shirt that provided adequate coverage of a plumber's rear, and a hilarious convention-defying marketing style. The company now trades on Wall Street under the ticker symbol DLTH, but Bob sold his stake back in the '90s. He wanted to be a dad, not a CEO.

When Max clamored for an allowance some years later, all this energy and experience (as if building up behind a dam) was ready to be poured into him.

Give a man a fish, and you feed him for a day. Teach a man to fish, and you feed him for a lifetime.

16-year-old Max and I crunched around his garden beds, atop a few inches of icy crust. 3,000 garlic cloves lay dormant below. Once grown into large, robust heads the following summer, they'd be cleverly packaged and marketed. The real money-maker was in his garlic salt, hand-crafted before dawn in a nearby restaurant's donated kitchen.

Max used the money from his business, Max Organics, to fuel a mountain biking addiction. An accomplished rider, he travelled a racing circuit. Racing-quality bikes aren't cheap. Garlic paved his way. Now in his 20s, he continues to ride. Growing superior garlic, however, is in the rearview mirror.

Visiting the Fierek's churned up intense turmoil, stirring envy for their unique educational approach. Homeschooling's flexibility afforded ample time for pursuing passions at a higher level. Max Organics taught him more life skills than any organized class. He also toured the country in a Volkswagen camper van, mountain bikes in tow. Opportunity, excitement, and business acumen rooted within a supportive home and family life.

I'm a stellar average dad. Like most of us, I want more for my kids. A scoffer might say, "Fierek cashed in his chips and is set for life. He and his wife can afford to invest more fully in their kids." While true to a point, it bears pointing out that Bob consciously chose moderate wealth, when he might have pressed into the stratosphere of excessive riches instead. We likewise have agency in our choices, and an ability to make sacrifices within our contexts. Even now, I must resolve to avoid the mire of self-doubt or depression in realizing how short I continue to measure up.

Your humble writer grew up in poverty, earned $40k at the time of his layoff, and now brings home significantly less while operating a growing business. We do, however, enjoy the tradeoff of free time. Since Shawna and I are in the thick of tuning our economic engines, we find it difficult to even approach the intentionality that Bob and his wife, Maria, invested into their kids. But, and it's a big but, we're trying.

Those early years of joblessness were pure survival mode. Even when we weren't working, achieving undistracted presence in family life was difficult. This has improved with time, but hasn't been easy. We're moving in a direction, and chose a simpler lifestyle over greater wealth. While failing to reach my God-like goals of fatherhood, I'm learning from mistakes and slowing down to take stock of small victories. Maybe that's enough.

Back to the Fierek's, Max's brother, Ben, tore into a massive set of Legos as I stepped into their large living area boasting a commanding view of the waterfront. The twelve-year-old helmed Ben's Blooms, an operation far more involved than you'd expect from a middle-schooler selling cut flowers.

His fresh blooms were a bright addition to the Whole Foods Co-op, and he was a force to be reckoned with over the holidays. His presence in the store was stunning: two full tables near the entrance loaded with some of the most unique, homespun gifts I've ever seen, all priced between $9.99 and $12.99. It was astonishing to observe that a 12-year-old boy had captured the most coveted display space at the height of Christmas season in a store that grossed over $16 million that year. Here were seed bomb kits, marimo ball kits, homemade ornaments, flower bulbs beautifully packaged atop Lake Superior rocks, and more.

I snatched up a bulb kit for my mother-in-law, reconnaissance for our January meeting. The gift was a big hit, bloomed for her in the dead of winter, and set me back $11.99. Later, referencing the attractive price points with Maria, I asked how much he was earning per unit. She hemmed and hawed evasively, so I asked, "A dollar?" Chuckling, she said, "Sometimes, but often not even that."

The point isn't the money, but lessons learned through marketing, merchandizing, packing, invoicing, bookkeeping, and everything else that goes into running a business. Also, in sharing garden space with his brother, the dynamic duo worked together by amending the soil through composting, crop rotation, etc.

I left their place with a gaggle of goodies that helped me absorb their clever marketing and packaging prowess: Vampire Garlic ("Perfect for keeping goblins away!"), garlic salt in a grinder (cherished daily until exhausted), a seed bomb kit, and a marimo ball pet (algae ball still grows in a jar on our windowsill). I laughed hysterically when Ben and Maria carried over a large container of 15-year-old specimens for me to handle, each the size of a tennis ball. Bizarre and beautiful, marimo balls are a bigger deal in Japan.

This encounter was profoundly challenging. Often sensing myself coasting as a parent, their example inspired me to instill a greater sense of responsibility and self-sufficiency in our kids. Wisdom is best imparted when applied holistically to all of life: mind, body, and soul.

The visit also got me wrestling. How might I earn a livelihood with and for my family? If children can operate a business, can't I? Later, I'd learn that running a business doesn't require a great deal of intellectual horsepower. It's more about grit, perseverance, paying attention, and desiring to benefit others.

Incidentally, all 14 of those garlic cloves plunged into the earth's crust in despair during an icy rain the month before would shoot forth in early spring, the first plants to emerge. The early greenery was a boost to mental health. I'd be ripe for change at that moment. Finally ready.

For now, it was still deep winter. These seeds, with all their potential, remained buried until the right conditions presented themselves. Still at a loss and depressed beyond words, hope was on the horizon. In darkness, the quest continued. Forward. Inch by inch.

29

Bottomless, unrelenting sadness wore heavy as I trudged down the steps to the Amazing Grace Cafe. There to extract a story about Gaelynn Lea, what I most needed was a friend. She'd arrive via elevator from her office a few floors up. On the eve of her 32nd birthday, Lea wasn't an internationally known commodity just yet. I caught up with Gaelynn on the cusp of her big break, which would arrive long before the snow melted.

Her means of navigating and perceiving the world diverges from the norm. This isn't merely reducible to her wheelchair, or the furtive glances cast her way whenever she enters a public space.

She glides in on a motorized wheelchair, like a magic carpet, approaches barista with empty mug, and hoists it upward with tiny hands and arms. Perhaps three times her size, he radiates honor in performing the simple task, as if doing so at the behest of a cherub—an angelic being who attends to God himself.

Employee carefully lowers hot ceramic with his head bowed to meet her gaze, sacred ritual now complete. Kindness and gentleness are conferred upon him through this act of service. It's apparent that familiarity between them has changed the 20-something fella.

Gaelynn manipulates joystick, chair pirouettes in a 180-degree turn, we make eye contact. As the gap closes between us, with a wry smile and eyes beaming with hope and humor, she is comfortable in her skin and bears a demeanor deflective of pity. With creativity, intelligence, vigor, and ableness packed into the slightest frame I've ever seen, I think, "She can't weigh much more than a 50-pound sack of grain."

Seen from a distance, one might view her as bent, misshapen, or even de-formed. Up close, in proper focus, her very being and presence on the planet seems informed, even obvious. Even as she needs, she is needed. Did God make a mistake? Her life, work, and way of being grant a fuller understanding of the oft-quoted lines of Psalm 139:

"For you created my inmost being;
You knit me together in my mother's womb.
I praise you because I am fearfully and wonderfully made;
Your works are wonderful,
I know that full well.
My frame was not hidden from you
When I was made in the secret place.
When I was woven together in the depths of the earth,
Your eyes saw my unformed body."

I suspect Gaelynn has laid hold of these words in a way I have not. This grappling has produced an overflow, a contribution impossible to replicate synthetically, for it was borne through struggle. Gaelynn's wrestling began in the womb, where 30 bones broke and healed into their current shape without cast or splint, a result of a genetic condition known as brittle bone disease. The current scorecard puts her at around 50 known breaks.

As Lea approached, there was no papering over my depression with feigned positivity. Wounded in plain sight, I was laid bare. My weakness, an inaudible yet ear-splitting cry, enabled a connection that otherwise might have eluded us. It wasn't just another interview. We connected as human beings. She immediately foraged for any available encouragement, help, or advice. Unusually confident and warm, Lea is the sort of person with whom one feels they may confide and arrive quickly at the heart of a matter.

I was at 40's threshold and nearly broke. Faint glimmers of career prospects had flamed out. It felt like others, through good looks, ample cash, and an easy manner, sailed through life effortlessly. Upon closer inspection, and a gaze away from my own navel, I came to see that very few people float through life with a charmed existence. Loneliness, sickness, struggle, and heartache visit us all.

Back in early 2016, weeks before being catapulted into fame, she had been hustling for years at the level of a busker. When out and about around town, you'd often find her performing at the smallest venues (farmers market, pizza place, coffee shop, any imaginable hole-in-the-wall) or opening for local musicians. Finally, after years of effort, one of her sparks caught the attention of a wider audience. Sitting there in the basement of the Dewitt Seitz building on that frigid January day, neither of us imagined she'd soon be opening for renowned bands like Wilco and the Decembrists, or would find herself composing original music for a Broadway production of Macbeth starring Daniel Craig, stationed at the center of the cultural radar.

Our point of connection became The Struggle. She was scratching out a living in those days. Half her income came from teaching fiddle lessons. $80 for five 30-minute lessons was an incredible bargain. Just 20% came from music gigs and album sales, and 30% from public speaking. She stared down mind-boggling challenges in a quest to make an independent living after abandoning Social Security's disability program, which has a way of encapsulating individuals into a life of poverty.

Paltry income limits force people into sham divorces. She chose marriage over "security." Her able-bodied husband, Paul, was then working as a janitor. Hearing her describe the dilemma made me recall my days as a collector for a credit card company (the compromise that landed a mortgage and an all-access pass to Cubicle Land). About every fifth call was a heartbreaking story of someone living a quiet life of despair in the disability system. Success meant a minimum payment that covered the interest, which, jacked up to 30%, resulted in a few precious dollars going to principle. Each and every one of them—thousands over a two-year stretch—treaded water indefinitely.

Gaelynn put a face on this subculture.

Interestingly, according to Department of Labor statistics, people with disabilities are twice as likely to start their own business than their able-bodied counterparts. Here's what Gaelynn has to say about the matter on her blog at violinscratches.com:

The reasons to go into business for one's self are no doubt varied. In my case, it was partly because the 9-5 working world was not conducive to someone who doesn't drive, has lots of doctor appointments, and takes forever to use the washroom. But I also made the switch because it's exciting to be the author of my own professional future, even if success isn't guaranteed. I love to create, and starting your own business makes this possible on almost every level.

On a more subtle level, perhaps having a disability forces you to get more comfortable with living outside the box. You're used to standing out in most situations, so why should one more societal difference be a big deal? Maybe in a society that doesn't really value accessibility (paying lip-service to "inclusion" or "acceptance" is different than actually building a ramp), you feel like to some extent you're always fending for yourself anyway. It might be less stressful and more fulfilling to fight your own battle on the periphery instead of working so hard to make it in the mainstream.

Lea sets a splendid example in pushing through challenges while leveraging talents to diversify income streams. She wasn't wholly reliant on any one thing. The possibility of being picked by gatekeepers never entered the equation. Gaelynn showed up every day, obstacles be damned.

This work ethic, in the face of comparatively impenetrable barriers, pricked me in the heart. As previously described, most days found me retrieving the mail in my pajamas at 9:30 am. Lea inspires me to try harder, and not give in to despair and difficulties, although, clad in pajamas, I finished her story in bed after lunch.

Maintaining an office outside the home was critical for Gaelynn. She calculated her 2015 income from music had come to a whopping $3.75/hour, so I guffawed at this arguably unnecessary expense.

Meeting my challenge, Lea asserted that the rent was worth every penny. In just one week's time, she'd prove it. Her big breakthrough might never have happened if she hadn't made this leap of faith. The office imposed a schedule, was reachable by public transportation, obliged her to dress appropriately, and provided a professional space for fiddle lessons. A workspace within a handicapped-accessible building housing numerous businesses and creatives was mentally stimulating, and a boon to her independence.

That evening, her husband, after finishing his second-shift job, would pick her up in an ancient minivan in the dead of night with snow swirling around in sub-zero temperatures. Two wood planks served as a ramp.

I accompanied her in the elevator to a cozy space on the fourth floor, where a girl in her tweens waited patiently, violin in hand. The brick wall with floor-to-ceiling windows boasting an impressive view of the bay seemed to encourage creative expression. In less than a week, at the end of a long day, she'd record her submission to National Public Radio's 2016 Tiny Desk Competition in this room while waiting for her husband. Late at night, being home might have meant watching Netflix, coasting toward bedtime. Instead, her big break was set into motion.

Lea, most improbably, won the competition and was ushered onto a national stage. Her humble entry—heart-stirring, soulful, honest, unabashed—beat out thousands of slick, MTV-like productions with action, intensity, and larger-than-life personalities. In a day and age where image is everything, Gaelynn (all three feet of her) is a breath of fresh air.

Held upright like a cello, her foot secures violin's base. Melody is called forth from some mysterious well. Top to bottom, her entire being—all spleen and all soul—settles into symbiotic rhythm with the instrument.

Might Gaelynn have been an object of pity prior to this conversation? She's remarkably resilient. Her incalculable value to society extends far beyond drawing awareness to accessibility issues. Lea's one-of-a-kind perspective and approach to problems stems from an uncommon life experience that can't help but enrich those around her.

Gaelynn helped me sink a deeper well into the courage required for moving forward into mystery. Her story altered my course, and will linger inside me forever.

Affording a fuller grasp of the very image of God, catching the briefest glimpse into a soul's unique contribution to culture's symphony is profoundly fulfilling.

There were others in the journey, but we must move along in our story. The effect of stacking encounters with characters beyond some perceived barrier—race, age, social class, disability, rural vs urban, far too many to list—will surprise you.

Act IV

Entering the Story

30

Stress levels reached new heights as I approached my 40th birthday, still without a clue of what to do with my life. Acid reflux made sleep fitful, forcing me out of bed before dawn. Despite the occasional blog post garnering admiration and attaboys from the community, but zero income, I was going nowhere fast. My project of befriending interesting people and writing about them was coming to an end. We needed income and stability. Even so, I reached into the bottom of the barrel to pay off our student loan debt 11 months early. The emotional cost of carrying it into this critical decade was too high.

I proudly counted myself among the 5% of Minnesotans, mostly elderly, confined to a landline. One of our working phones, in fact, has an actual bell in it (Grandma's old rotary). I scoffed at the hordes of humanity, staring at their gizmos and missing out on the real world.

But, when my ancient digital camera broke just prior to

my meeting with incoming Mayor, Emily Larson, I sent an SOS into the world in search of another. A neighbor agreed to part with her iPhone 4 in exchange for four beers. After placing a new battery into the device, I had a working camera, while chuckling that I was like a four-year-old getting Mom's old phone so I could snap photos. I used the point-and-shoot for several months without considering other capabilities. Wasn't even curious.

It was the dreariest sort of day, classic early spring in Duluth—rain driven by high winds off the Lake at 35 degrees, pooling and running off a sheet of ice—weather designed to cull the herd of dead weight like me. I spent day after day scrubbing walls and woodwork, priming and painting. Filthy floors beneath me were littered with old nails, dirt, sawdust, and construction debris. The carpenter, not wishing to be outdone, completed the witch's brew by evacuating his bowels in the unvented bathroom (destroying the toilet) prior to leaving for the day. Hermetically sealed house stewed in sewage for hours. Adding insult to injury, all day radio listening had become boring. My brain needed diversion.

Shawna suggested I get into podcasts.

"What's a podcast?"

Sensing a need to show rather than tell, adopting the technique of a middle-aged daughter with an elderly father, she pulled up the app on my "camera." Somehow, miraculously perhaps, I stumbled upon the Urban Farmer Podcast, featuring Curtis Stone. After just two listens, I found something tangible to pursue. Curtis demonstrated that not owning land, or the burden of its accompanying debt, can be a strength.

My love for farming was validated as a bonafide career choice for the first time.

A few months earlier, while discussing my layoff and journey through the wilderness, Emily Larson asked what kind of work I was looking for. After hemming and hawing for an uncomfortably long time, I stammered out, "I dunno, but it has to be something rooted in the community." This conversation came to mind as urban farming rose to the surface, an answer that seemed about as sudden as a crush on a beautiful girl. Upon reflection, however, a lengthy pilgrimage had led here. I was finally ready to make the leap. My quest to integrate our family into a hyper-local economy could be realized through an option hiding in plain sight.

Shawna has long prevented us from fleeing the city for the country. This intractable problem, ironically, was the solution. Her refusal to move out to real acreage is the reason I could spin an irrational farm dream—something that stalked me from at least the age of six—into reality. The beauty of SPIN farming (Small Plot Intensive) is its low barrier to entry. Half a million dollars for land and expensive equipment are no longer prerequisites. With minuscule overhead costs, profit margins dwarf those massive operations involving combines and silos.

Armed with two hours of podcast conversations about this style of agriculture, I popped in unannounced at church during a staff meeting. Eyes appeared glazed over during a discussion of something tedious and soulless, like insurance. Clad in dirty painter whites, I arrived as a breath of fresh air. The church owned a house with a large yard near the main facility, which I proposed to transform into the flagship plot of my urban farm. Associate pastor clapped his hands and burst out laughing. I presented the following business plan, arms gesticulating wildly in enthusiastic agreement:

1. Put some seeds in the ground.
2. Grow food.
3. Sell it.

Following a few days of deliberation, they granted me the land in exchange for mowing the lawn. Immediately, prior to conjuring up any complicated contract, I invested $137 in 4,000 square feet of black plastic for smothering the sod. This was my first capital expenditure.

Locally Laid, a mid-sized laying hen operation, in contrast, practically had to sell their souls to access water on rented land by punching a well deep into the earth's crust to the tune of $16,000. At an estimated $0.25 wholesale price per egg, that's 64,000 eggs just to pay for the water. Chickens lay a single egg about every 25 hours, so that's some interesting math.

Farmers routinely take this sort of investment for granted, one among many, as necessary for entering the game. You've got to pay to play. I, on the other hand, had access to tap water through a household spigot located 15 feet from my first big rectangle.

That first night was a doozy. High winds whipped up Lake Superior as waves devastated the shoreline a half-mile away. There weren't enough rocks in the world to hold down the plastic. What a nightmare! Twice daily, or thrice, I visited my patch of petroleum to find it flapping wildly in the breeze. Seaming together two giant pieces of plastic, each measuring 100 feet by 20, with every rock or log I could find, the massive sails transformed into something like those twisting inflatable dancing figures outside car dealerships. I sauntered into church 15 minutes late each Sunday, after placing more weight atop the twin sails. Heavy tarps beneath sandbags are a better choice.

I just saved you a month of frustration, by the way.

The following month, in a hurry to get started, I rented a sod-cutter. I've got a crazy picture of hundreds of rolls of sod taken by that camera/podcasting gizmo, and I have no memory of what we did with these thousands of pounds of material. Scraping off the grass was only the beginning, and this meant removing way too much precious topsoil, leaving mostly dense clay. Rocks came in astounding numbers and quality, many of which required levering from holes and rolling away. Rock & roll!

Land preparation proceeded with the addition of compost and other amendments, aeration with a hand tool known as a broad fork, and endlessly moving tarps in and out of position.

With the benefit of hindsight, it's ridiculous to launch a farm business in the spring. Nonsensical, in fact. That first season should be devoted to preparing the land. All I could do, once the weeds started proliferating, was tread water to keep from drowning. By the month of June, it was obvious that Tiny Farm Duluth would remain a side hustle for 2016. I was working three jobs—farmhand at an established farm for further experience, house-painting, and building a farm from scratch—from sunup to sundown.

That first season, moving largely by bicycle, I delivered fresh produce to a handful of supportive families, toting around $5 - $20 deliveries of greens, radishes, beans, and whatnot in a cooler. I grossed a thousand bucks. This obligated me to file a Schedule F (form for farms) on our taxes, which later proved crucial for future success.

Lacking the ability to even dream about moving to the country to give farming a go, "someday," I went for it with the resources available to me. The conundrum of having no land, or even a distant future hope for any, became the solution to turning a lifelong dream into reality.

Limitation is the mother of creativity.

I hoped to build a family life rooted in the riches of land and community, staking out a small space at the intersection of economy, community, and ecology. Meaningful economic exchange between neighbors is critical. Without it, you lose all three.

The publication of my book resulted in amazing feedback, but it was frustrating to have no additional products for my small crowd of loyal fans. It was, and is, exciting to work toward a high-quality consumable product that enticed customers to return week after week.

Failure was no longer a fear. Failing to try, lost in analysis paralysis, is a recipe for stagnation. In this, I was an expert. Vast reservoirs of energy, stored up inside me, flowed into the work. Any remaining veneers of normalcy or outward signs of success sloughed off. There simply wasn't time for putting on airs.

When Shawna kicked off an exhibition at a nearby art gallery, conveniently located between a painting project and home, I showed up as I was during a lunch break. In the photograph, Shawna is all dolled up in pretty clothes and perfectly coiffed hair, while I'm bedecked in filthy painter pants and blaze orange hunting cap. Two dozen pieces, mostly from her Land of Wonder series, hang in the background.

She was supportive of the whole thing. This is what tilling tough new ground looks like in the beginning, and my, was it ever liberating. Unshackled from convention, we pressed forward together with the assets at our disposal. Our operations were all profitable, but as bootstrapped as you can get. Between painting houses, book sales, "farming," and Shawna's artwork, we cleared just under $20,000 in profit that year. Pretty nuts, huh?

Seeds were being sown toward a more sustainable future, as both our businesses were on the cusp of major breakthroughs. It'd be a mighty long row to hoe in the meantime. This wasn't about brains or brilliance, but simple grit. Moving forward and showing up, day after day.

31

Only the clinically insane, ignorant, or desperate, should launch a farm business in spring. All at once, all your ducks need to be in a row. A plan for succession planting must not only be contemplated, but in force. Seeds go into the ground every week. Systems, such as an irrigation strategy (overhead sprinklers vs drip tape), should already be in place and operational. Similarly, weeds should be manageable as a minor annoyance through stale seedbed techniques. Problem is, in the beginning, you barely understand any of this. There's almost no intuition to guide the inexperienced farmer through a barrage of decisions and actions.

With a to-do list exceeding available time and knowledge, I rose with the birds without an alarm clock. At 3:45 am, I was walking with my head down and deep in thought, rushing between chicken chores and heading out, when a tiny tree sapling caught my eye inside our fire pit.

With way too many front-burner issues—chaos in all

quadrants—there wasn't a spare moment for ruminating on my time poverty.

Instead of rushing off at the behest of the hardest taskmaster I've ever known, myself, I studied the diminutive box elder tree. Firmly rooted on a piece of charred wood, I marveled at its resilience. I spent five minutes with the little guy and potted him up. Our time together recharged my battery with hope and inspiration. It was the first moment of stopping in quite a while. Momentum irresistibly propelled me forward at all times. Willpower was required to hit the brakes, stop, rest, and reflect. It called to mind a chapter in my book, and life, called "Joy in the Journey," which began with a sentence describing life on the train:

Riding the rails is a feast along a bountiful reservoir of time.

Though one of my longest days lay ahead, these few minutes sacrificed in awe of unexpected beauty set me on a mission to recover this mentality. Ironically, we become more productive while existing within a state of awe, enchantment, and gratitude. Intense clarity burns off the fog, enabling greater focus on core essentials and a surprising ability to embrace challenging circumstances.

With my head in the right place—renewed, expanded, and ripe for enchantment—I hopped on my bike, en route to plant beans and attend to as many fires as possible on what suddenly felt like a not-so-tiny farm plot. From there I'd pedal to the other farm eight miles away, where I worked as a farmhand. Afterward, on the way home, I'd set the stage for painting a house the following day, racking up 20 miles on the bike. Time, so scarce and precious, spent on the bike while passing through the countryside was mentally, physically, and spiritually rewarding. I resolved to be pleased that the family car was unavailable, uncovered joy in the journey, and refused to regret the many things left unaccomplished that day.

I envied the 20-year-old embarking on a journey through apprenticeships or similar hard knocks, but without family responsibilities. At 40 years old, at least I was finally getting started. While the best time to plant a tree was 20 years ago, the second best is today. Experience showed that there's time enough for accomplishing everything needing to get done.

Standing in the shower that evening, I marveled at the extremely dirty water pooling up in the tub. The runoff was quite the contrast to the pristine wastewater that poured off me between tours of duty at the office! The day was far from over, but this was a joyous occasion. I stuffed my feet back into the same tattered shoes worn in the field and raced Shawna to the opening of her art exhibition at The Red Herring Lounge (the venue that hosted Cornucopia displayed her unique surrealism for a full month). What an enjoyable reprieve from those daylight hours, stooped beneath intense sunshine. Unlike the farm, house painting, and aggressive bookselling, I sat back and enjoyed Shawna's talents without being responsible for her success. It was marvelous.

32

It isn't every day that vinyl arrives in the mail directly from the record label. Not just any record, but a limited edition release from your favorite musician on the planet. And not just any old favorite musician, but a good friend. And, the biggest AND at that, Shawna painted the album's visual artwork. Like an engorged tick, I nearly burst with joy while lapping up this once-in-a-lifetime experience.

Charlie Parr vetoed the original painting. He grows weary of seeing his distinctive face—aging, bearded, shrouded by scraggly hair—placed on nearly everything he puts out.

Out of the blue, as Shawna prepared to paint over it, Charlie called to say the Label wanted this image on the cover. Time was of the essence.

In a matter of minutes, she would have brushed it out of existence.

It's a marvelous piece of surrealism. Smile and laugh

lines curve down into the familiar beard, which transforms into a stump and roots. He's planted in the forest, a refuge for flora and fauna.

Charlie contented himself with having Shawna paint the bear he may have preferred on the back of his iconic, steel resonator guitar. It's a real beaut. More recently, he has signed with Smithsonian Folkways Recordings, the same label that husbands the works of icons like Woody Guthrie and Lead Belly. Do you suppose I may have plunked around on his guitar while we had it over here? Find the photos on my webpage.

Shawna had kept at it, grinding away for years in obscurity, perfecting her craft. To the rest of the world, it was as if she had come out of nowhere. Her rising star was never a surprise to me. It was, and is, only a matter of time. After all that unsung dedication, she was ready to put out her best work when amazing opportunities finally came her way.

Symbiosis between art forms is exhilarating. Synergistically, talents as divergent as east from west conjoin in partnership, creating a yield greater than the sum of their parts. We are stronger together than if our efforts floundered around on their own.

The farm feeds and strengthens her business, which, in turn, nourishes my work. All of it—farm, art, writing—enmesh and reinforce one another as legs of a single stool upon which our family rests. Together.

Meanwhile, Shawna booked exhibitions all over the place, which led to a permanent gallery presence in Minneapolis, and then on East and West coasts. Her reach has grown slowly and organically. Commitments stretch her to grow incrementally, but never outstrip her abilities. There has never been one big break where some larger than life social media personality promoted her work to the stratosphere. Lindsey Lohan's brother reached out privately regarding some work hanging in Palm Springs, which was pretty cool for novelty's sake, but certainly wasn't a golden ticket to "making it."

As expensive as fine art hanging in a prestigious gallery may be, gas station attendants are comparatively flush with cash. Our modus operandi has always been to keep cranking out work. Opportunities for greater exposure grow in tandem with increasing abilities.

Her work comprises roughly half our income, with the farm providing the rest. This is the secret sauce! So, as I edit this book and hustle it out of our computer and into your hands at a time of year when demand for the farm's products decrease, Shawna may sell an additional painting. Her sales naturally pick up as mine drop off, causing me to accept the seasonality of farm sales as natural and positive.

The tables have turned. Shawna encourages me to write without regard for sales, just as I pushed her years ago to produce work from an overflowing heart. She believes in me as I have always believed in her. We have freedom to create. While our net pay remains in the low 30 thousands, these income streams aren't overly stressed. We only count on them for achievable revenue.

Years of struggle and sacrifice were required for "arriving" here. Back in 2016, little things like having the mayor select one of Shawna's paintings for her office, where it continues to hang quietly on loan, felt extraordinarily significant. Just knowing it's there, providing enjoyment and satisfaction for a harried chief executive, is a source of encouragement. Every now and again, on rare occasions when we see the TV news, we'll see it in the background. Quiet moments like this, noticeable only to us, are awesome.

33

Lunch on the elderly farmer's porch was sacred. Three days a week I worked alone in the pickle lady's fields and greenhouses (planting, harvesting, and maintaining fence lines) as she labored tirelessly in her commercial kitchen, cranking out jar after jar. When the moment finally arrived, I nestled into a chair on the coolly shaded veranda, liberated sweaty feet from confining work boots, and savored every bite.

My nourishment was the fruit of the prior year's labor, cost me dearly, and came to be worth every ounce of sweat equity poured into it. Who knew a simple sandwich could be so satisfying?

The price tag on this turkey came in at a whopping $90. By my reckoning, the cost was higher: twelve hours of hard labor for Janaki at the Food Farm. That time had passed—joyfully, mostly— beneath a blistering sun, amidst relentless wind, and in endurance of damp cold at season's end. This wasn't like trading a dozen hours of Netflix-viewing. I earned it.

Was 12 hours a fair exchange for a pasture-raised bird? When I agreed to take the extra turkey, I assumed it might cost half as much. If I had inquired about how much it came to, I surely would've declined, robbing myself of an exercise that went on for many months.

Was it worth it?

Initially regretting my foolishness, I plunged the 26-pound bird into the freezer for six months, unable to deal with it. Later, after tiptoeing into pastured poultry myself and coming to understand the process and costs involved, I rescued the giant protein capsule from suspended animation.

I turned to my friend Matt to ensure its thoughtful and artful preparation. He's the sort of chap who lives for roasting a pig, smoking meat all day long, or curing it the old-fashioned way by hanging hundreds of dollars of it in the garage for weeks or months at a time. If anyone could give this bird its due, it was him. Matt roasted it to perfection, slowly, after a good long brining. Afterwards, I carefully broke it down into small, manageable packages for slow, deliberative consumption.

While our family shared a generous portion around the table, I seem to most cherish those memories of enjoying it in the oasis of that shaded porch, where I savored every bite. I considered the life that was given so I might live, feeling gratitude for my specific turkey. It had lived as a turkey should, expressing its innate turkeyness until its last breath. In the fullness of time, my 12 hours of mediocre, wannabe-farmer labor arrived at a remarkable bargain. Did it even compare to this bird's sacrifice?

Every day became an opportunity to express thanksgiving. Begrimed in sweat and dirt from working in and upon the earth, I became grateful for every mouthful. This was worth $3.50/pound, and then some.

These turkeys are raised to be the centerpiece of a family's

Thanksgiving dinner. Would anything less befit an annual celebration of everything the Maker has provided? On this, of all days, it behooves us to source food grown in a manner in which it was designed to be grown, while simultaneously sharing our abundance with growers in our own communities.

In stark contrast to the industrial practice of raising conventional poultry—thousands of debeaked birds confined within a single building (never seeing the light of day) in filthy conditions that require an overdose of antibiotics, and thus contribute to the rise of superbugs that may herald the end of the antibiotic era—Janaki's turkeys spend 22 weeks on pasture while foraging on healthy grass, upon which I have walked. Farmhands move their portable pens to fresh grass every day, where they're monitored twice daily.

And, holy cow, is their feed ever expensive. Food Farm's farmer-in-chief pays more than twice the rate per pound for his organically grown grain than what you'd shell out at your local feed store for a 50-pound sack of conventional feed, even though he hauls in a thousand pounds at a time! He has kelp and minerals added to it as well. Janaki says, "Stuff like that gives the meat more of the healthy fats and less of the bad. It also makes for a healthier bird that can handle being out in the elements and stay alive for a longer period of time."

Finally, I think of Laura, the delightfully whimsical farmhand who was glad to be with the turkeys at the end. One by one, they were selected for "processing." As their numbers dwindled, she cried.

Most of us cannot afford to eat like this every day of the year. Janaki certainly can't justify growing that much. But, it's worthy of a little reflection from time to time, even if only one day per year, particularly that which has the potential to transport us to the very brink of the holy. Is this level of gratitude and joy possible after stooping to select a frozen bundle from a supermarket's freezer case?

Though my relationship with it came via happy accident, I was blessed by months of rumination on this single being's contribution to my life. Thank you kindly, Meleagris gallopavo domesticus.

34

The bitch died in my arms.

She had been in miserable shape all day. The smell of death was overwhelming. Placing the animal outside drew the attention of every fly in the Western Hemisphere. Shawna begged me to come home early from the farmhand job, but I was busy with that day's harvest.

After repeated pleas from my wife, I finally rushed home to face the inevitable. During lunch on the farmer's porch, I called to make arrangements. Perhaps uncouth, I asked for a quote of costs for euthanasia, cremation, etc. At nine bucks an hour, this is just how it is. Resignedly accepting whatever bill they hand you in the end isn't an option.

My plan was to drop the dog off at the clinic to have her euthanized, give a quick hug, and hustle off. Ten minutes later I'd be high atop a ladder finishing a paint job, arriving home with a fistful of cash at dark. Poverty has a way of putting ridiculous notions into your head.

Tillie waited for me all day, barely hanging on. She summoned every bit of energy to stand and greet me one last time. Then she collapsed, lost consciousness, and faded away in my arms. A few more shallow breaths, and she was gone. All in about three minutes. The family dog, who adored me above all, endured horrific suffering throughout the longest day of her life, only to greet me one last time. Now that's devotion.

A dog dying in your arms knocks some sense into you. Death is never convenient.

Instead of rushing off to that job, I grabbed a shovel. Resisting tears, I drenched her grave with sweat on a scorcher of a day. There was nothing left to do. Difficult work, it was really cathartic.

Sinking a three-foot-wide hole four feet into stubborn red clay (as far as I could go) takes a lot out of a guy. Nothing about death is easy, and it shouldn't be.

Wrapped in a burial shroud, Tillie was placed into a cardboard casket fashioned from our endless supply of boxes. Together with my wife and kids, we lowered her deep into the cool earth, just a few feet away from the couch in our living room where we often snuggled. It's comforting to know she's out there to this day, still close to her pack. This knowledge brings me to tears, even now. I barely understand it, but grief can be such a gift.

The kids made a note of favorite memories and a bouquet of flowers, adding marvelous contrast to the earth's interior. They completed the burial by filling the hole back in atop their beloved pet, receiving closure through this simple act.

It was beautiful. Healing even. The children dealt with the loss remarkably well. None of it was supposed to happen this way. She was only a few years old. Strangely, I cannot think of a more positive outcome.

I came terribly close to robbing our family of a cherished memory. A brief handoff at the clinic would have been a minor interruption in a busy life that continued on unabated.

Instead, everything came to a halt. We spent the night in, huddled up, sharing tears and even a few laughs, reminiscing. The family banded together to process grave loss as best we could. Somehow, despite myself, we handled this really well simply because we were all a part of it.

Two years after my layoff, losses continued piling up. In the days leading up to the dog's premature death, I was feeling sorry for us. Afterward, not so much. Life resembled a sad, old-time country song following the loss of friendships, broken appliances, financial upheavals, distress, and now this. Ironically, this bereavement put life into greater perspective, causing us to cling to blessings that remained.

Death, or any significant loss, isn't something to handle clinically, somehow sealed off in an airtight container. Wholly other.

Time stopped.

We walked through grief together. The painting project—a thousand bucks ripe and ready—could wait. Accumulating cash as an end in and of itself is almost always the wrong choice.

It's fascinating to see, and to have felt so viscerally, how money inserts itself into most decisions. Short-term expediency produces poor choices, or, perhaps more accurately, wayward navigation. A short supply of money sets surprisingly fruitful limits, presuming we rest within these boundaries, alert for the next guidepost.

Arriving at a solution, instead of imposing one, is perhaps the most unexpected discovery throughout this turbulent period. Much of life is outside our control. It's utterly unreal to discover how little power we have to determine our future. And yet, we have agency. It's as if we are helmeted in a kayak, enjoying the ride while pivoting and turning to avoid dangerous rocks. Rather than fight the current, I've learned to flow downstream as the river carries us along. This is marvelously freeing.

Our handling of the dog's death lives on as a favorite memory. My obvious lack of control over the situation and inability to shield the kids from painful reality, was, and is, exquisite. Despite my many failings, we arrived at a solution that was far and away more beautiful and healing than anything I could have concocted. We'd arrive at greater solutions to more complex problems in time, many of which exceeded abilities or resources. Resting within our boundaries, we learned to wait.

35

Time for reveling in enlightenment was short. The Grim Reaper was busy that evening. The timing of it all pointed toward Ultimate Choreography.

The incomplete digestion of pain and disappointment underlies, for many, an abandonment of hope. Even after laying mayhem's responsibility at God's feet, I discovered the opposite. Extreme adversity furnishes opportunity for faith's deepening.

Who or what is the object of faith and hope? Is it a comfortable life with tangible earthly blessings, or the Being who holds all things together?

Phone calls like the one waking me at first light the morning after our dog died became routine. In the dead of night, on idyllic pasture just outside town, a mysterious gang of predators made off with 80+ chickens. With a notable absence of blood and gore, I snapped a photo of the only shred of evidence at the crime scene: a well-worn path leading to the forest.

Matt and I were trialing our first run of a hundred meat chickens. $1900 of pastured poultry vanished through a small hole, six feet in the air, at the top of our chicken tractor prototype. This wasn't chump change for a family that would earn ten times that for an entire year of work.

Devastating.

Tragic, life-altering events help shape us. How we handle them sets the tone for the next stage of our lives. We must live fully in and through the moment, even prior to the wound's coagulation."Why me?" is a question best avoided. Death and loss come to us all. What we do with it, in large measure, forges our character.

Our family racked up devastations at such an alarming rate that each day's setbacks ceased to surprise me. They were vivid lessons that we do not possess the people, places, and things gracing our lives.

We are not in control.

Long ago, at my entry point into Cubicle Land, I worked in collections for a credit card company. At 8 am in the Bronx, Christmas Eve included, the client picks up the phone from their bedside.

"Hello?"

"Good morning Mr. Jones. You have a balance due of $15,321. Can you pay that today?"

An unending laundry list of excuses made me ask myself, "How can one person have so much drama in their life?"

Now, I could finally relate.

Resilience, grit, and gratitude don't happen automatically. They are a byproduct of pain, as with cataclysmic tectonic forces pushing forth mountains.

Our losses went on to include friendships, a car engine AND transmission, farm land upon which we had staked the next season's income, ALL our appliances from the toaster to the refrigerator and water heater, the dog, our home's roof, my job, ad infinitum. I had to stop keeping track and simply accept.

A good crisis, one not wasted, is an opportunity for growth. Our family rallied through these events like never before, learning to muster up the courage to walk through them. Together. There's no going around these life-altering storms, wishing them away, or burying heads in the sand. We must walk straight through them, and by doing so, we learn that when the worst case scenario actually happens, it's manageable. The worst thing that can happen isn't the end of the world. It's an opportunity.

And so, like digging that hole, I simply did the obvious. There wasn't time for feeling sorry for myself, or to brood over how I failed to protect our grubstake. I shuttled 11 surviving chickens back to our home in the city, where I'd move them to a fresh space in our small yard every day.

This required complex choreography, because we already tended a backyard flock of laying hens, a pair of ducks, and five young ducklings. All this poultry was getting ridiculous. Our libido-rich drake was working out his hormones on the chickens. We joked about hatching a cross of chucks or dickens. After moving the ducks to a less secure location, we temporarily had four individual flocks. The backyard was chaos.

Raccoons visited every evening. Quacking ducks roused me from bed in the dead of night. Arriving just in time on one occasion, the predator was dragging the hen by her neck. Fat raccoon awkwardly scrambled up the fence empty-pawed, stymied by the sleep-deprived farmer yet again.

Meanwhile, the market garden was a gong show of weeds after suffering irreparable storm damage. A house painting project dragged on forever, because I spared only a couple hours at a time. I was spread too thin.

Harrowing times were essential for learning how to fail. And, after failing, I needed to develop courage for failing again. The alternative was a return to the cubicle, where failure had been gradual, like a frog slowly boiling in a comfortable pot. For a high-achiever like me—one skilled at taking tests, writing essays, an A-student who performed admirably when directed by a boss—this was a painful lesson. I was a mediocre, beginner farmer.

Ok, that's an overly optimistic assessment.

Perseverance and grit can be cultivated. Once grown into your life, failures like these become seeds for ultimate success.

Loss of income was only the tip of the iceberg when grieving the disappearance of nearly seven dozen chickens. This venture had grown into a repository of tremendous energy and hope over the preceding month.

I was just as excited as those 100 chicks while collecting them at 6 am from the post office. They all arrived alive and vigorous 24 hours after hatching. What a miracle! Baby chicks seem designed for shipping by U.S. Mail. Slurping down the yolk just prior to hatching, they have all the nutrition necessary to sustain them for three days without food or water. Two large, ventilated boxes produced such a cacophony of chirping that they seemed to contain all the birds of the forest. So much potential, hope, and excitement. Energy!

Optimism and joy marked those first 18 hours. The chicks—tiny, adorable, yellow fluff balls— went into a 64-square foot brooder in the garage, where classical music serenaded them. My partner in the chicken operation, Matt, dipped his beak into the effort as a side project. We were both skilled at raising backyard flocks, but 100 chicks demand more intensive management. The car was booted from its place of prominence, and I doted on them. Everything was perfect.

Until it wasn't.

The most violent storm in decades hit Duluth on the first night of our joint business venture. 90+ mile-per-hour winds destroyed much of the electrical grid, leaving the power out for days. Hours later, I discovered the chicks huddled together, desperately chilled without supplemental heat. There was no time to think. Just do the work. Through some miracle, I hadn't crushed the boxes they arrived in, so I boxed them up and placed them upstairs beside a roaring woodstove. It was surreal to stoke such heat on a July day that would later reach 95 degrees, but you do what you've got to do. No matter how prepared you are, there are forces outside your control that can derail the best intentions and preparation.

Major effort went into the next three weeks until the chicks feathered out and were ready to move outside. Everybody went for a slow ride from the city to the country in a large trailer atop a soft bed of hay as we made our way to pasture. This was great, foolish fun. So much hope!

I was grateful to have a business partner on the protein side of Tiny Farm Duluth. Large, arduous tasks became fun, because I wasn't in them alone. Driving home from the farm supply store, for example, was hilarious. The trailer took on the form of a Conestoga wagon with 16-foot-long cattle panels bent into an arch, drawing onlookers like a parade float on our journey home across back roads.

Hoping to scale things up if this trial run succeeded, we found pleasure in putting nuts and bolts of the operation together. We even scouted out sites for raising pastured pigs and sheep, feeling hopeful for its viability as a business.

Those 11 surviving chickens used every patch of grass in my yard, which was blessed with a large schmear of high-nitrogen crap with every move of their quarters. Rats descending upon the yard en masse felt like an outward manifestation of inner chaos. (Most unfortunately, a nearby road project had expelled the rodents from sewers into our neighborhood.)

Stress on our small property forced us to move the birds back to their chicken tractor after patching the hole, an opportunity to test out newly reinforced accommodations with minimal risk.

In the end, we proved to ourselves that it worked. Also, we could sell the birds at a high price per pound. Since I filed taxes for Tiny Farm Duluth showing revenue, I could speak intelligently and confidently about a proposed expansion of veggie and chicken operations, and thus secured a $10,000 loan from the USDA for the following season. And, against all odds, I was granted entrance to the Duluth Farmers Market. Failure provided grist for future success and clarity.

The following spring, I emerged as a battle-tested warrior with war stories and the scars to prove them. Regular day to day problems associated with launching a business became a matter of routine. I had already run the gauntlet. These I could handle.

36

750 days after my firing, with every iron withdrawn from the fire, we returned to the crossroads.

The last painting project, a series of garages at the Materials Recovery Center, was complete. Eager to make hay before winter, I spent two solid weeks out there. After all the people and vehicles drove off, locking me in behind the closed gate with the fleet of heavy equipment finally asleep, the expansive sky grew into a source of wonder. A peaceful hush descended. Beauty unfurled, under the impression nobody saw its true form. A respectful admirer from a distance, I adored it.

In contrast to some dignitary receiving a ceremonial key to the city, I had a working key to the dump. Answerable only to the weather, my access was complete. Then, the project ended. Now what?

We butchered the 11 surviving meat chickens that consumed far too much time and attention. On a crisp fall day, I collected the last bird. As heads rolled 15 feet in the distance, she calmly sat in the grass with a contemplative aspect, content and at peace. I gathered her up with little fuss.

"Thank you for your life, darling…"

Animal husbandry has been a passion since childhood, when 50 birds flew freely in my bedroom above a kingdom of critters both terrestrial and aquatic. Unable to pursue my romanticized notion of a rural farm, I was determined to live out the ethos of a country farmer as much as possible. I even spent a few minutes in conversation with farm hero, Joel Salatin, at an agricultural conference. Neither the President, Bob Dylan, or some sports figure, could have meant as much. If you had asked me about meeting one person, living or dead, this was the pinnacle. Of incalculable influence in the local agriculture movement, you might know him from the groundbreaking documentary, Food Inc, or from Michael Pollan's book, The Omnivore's Dilemma.

I strove to raise meat chickens, and eventually other animals, in a manner similar to his style of moving them to fresh grass every day. It's a multifaceted, management-intensive choreography of cows, pigs, and chickens. While simultaneously healing the land and sequestering carbon in the soil, the nutrition profile dwarfs anything coming off a factory farm's assembly line. Though I could only aspire to bits and bobs of his strategy upon a borrowed patchwork of properties, becoming increasingly impractical from a distance, the attempt was rewarding.

All at once, time opened as wide as the horizon. I went from 80 to 100 hours a week, body reaching its limits, to absolutely nothing. This is a more difficult transition than one might realize.

I had been far too busy finishing the paint job before the weather turned, harvesting the last of my market garden, demonstrating proof of concept for the chickens, and finishing the farmhand work, to contemplate anything afterward. It was as if the bullet train stopped on a dime, depositing me at those familiar crossroads.

On the very evening of my last paid gig, at Pickle Lady's place, I reluctantly attended a theatre production at the University of Minnesota Duluth featuring an Eddy Gilmore character. Expecting nothing but indigestion, I stepped inside thinking, "I guess I have nothing better to do."

Blessed by an atmosphere of utter richness, I left with more wealth than could be hauled away in pockets, wheelbarrows, or armored trucks. Taking in the play, One River, on this particular night when all economic prospects had been extinguished for the season, made for exquisite timing.

It was on a par with the unexpected beauty of Tillie dying in my arms two months earlier during our final greeting. If the entirety of my experience with the animal had been distilled into that one precious moment of her passing, the time and treasure devoted to her would have been worthwhile.

This singular moment of infinite time, within a small theatre where it was impossible to slink away into obscurity, felt similarly inserted into my life. Supernaturally.

We made eye contact almost instantly. He clearly recognized me. Feeling unbelievably uncomfortable, there was no possibility of disappearing into an audience of a hundred.

You can't get away with shoddy, insincere acting in such an environment. Luke Harger, who played Eddy and several other roles, never lost a beat. While I would have succumbed to self-consciousness, Luke and the rest of the cast continued emoting powerfully. Each of them had their own doppelgängers in the audience on opening night and were equally emptied of insecurities.

I've written vulnerably—19 years of bedwetting being the least of which—but I've never laid myself as bare as these actors. Their souls were exposed, a nakedness in public I find unimaginable.

This may have been the most passionate, dialed in group of college students I've ever witnessed. They were doing what they love, liberated from discussion of techniques or theory. These kids weren't just preparing for a nebulous future, waiting to be chosen, but were doing it now. The concept, so simple, is extraordinary; something to emulate. Their collective passion and thrill produced a remarkable chemistry between cast members, evident on stage and off. This formula for success is what I'm after in life and in community. To be reminded of this on stage, amid such confusion, was marvelous beyond description.

Harger captured me at my very best, the part I stumble into during moments of sublimity.

I thought Tom Isbell, the playwright and director of One River, was crazy for taking on a community project called One River, Many Stories, because it lacked any structure or form. Over the course of the previous year, journalists and storytellers across all mediums were encouraged to share stories about the St. Louis River, Lake Superior's largest U.S. tributary.

An important part of our history, the river has been overlooked for decades. Duluth's raw sewage was pumped directly into the estuary until the 1970s, along with every conceivable industrial effluent. The location of the steel mill referenced in Bob Fierek's origin story, for example, is an ongoing Superfund site. Visitors and residents alike have historically ignored the river, en route to the many pleasures afforded by the Big Lake containing 10% of the world's fresh water.

Hundreds of stories were submitted, as storytellers and journalists went around doing their thing, interacting with thousands of years of history. While beautiful and often interesting, it was anarchy. The idea of crafting a cohesive story out of all this mess was ridiculous. And yet, through some mysterious alchemy, he captured the essence. The play captivated the hearts of audiences far beyond the St. Louis River watershed, earning four national awards in the process.

Not only did Isbell choose my story as something to dramatize among several other highlights telling stories of river and community, he pulled ideas and quotes from it to provide necessary structure to the overall production. It became a kind of skeleton for holding it all together. The performance even concluded with a summary quote from my humble blog post:

I poured a lot of myself into understanding, and into actually entering this one little portion of the Story. Without a sense of place there is no story. Without a story, there is no sense of place. Wherever you live, I urge you to enter into that story. Delight in sharing it with others. Become part of it. Help to shape it, as even now the story is being passed along to the next generation. It's always in motion. Rather than fight the current, perhaps use it to help shape the contours of a narrative continually in the process of being written, even at this very moment...

Observing the process of literally entering this story, dramatized on stage a dozen feet from me, was deeply moving. As nebulous a notion as this was, and is, I left with a deep sense that this was the direction I must take.

Contributing to the community effort intimidated me, and I had no relationship with the Louie. I attended a meeting on a cold February evening, featuring admired luminaries as guests panelists (the local outdoors writer, Minnesota Public Radio correspondent, and a successful author). Everyone in the room was bona fide. I was an unemployed wannabe writer attempting to blog his way out of a midlife crisis. While enjoying the free beer, I puzzled over what my contribution might be.

I imagined arriving just in the nick of time to the next meeting at a local brewery in late March. Like a nervous kid entering a crowded school cafeteria, I'd have to find my place among a mob of successful people.

As luck would have it, ice-out came early that year, occurring on March 29th in the St. Louis River estuary, the very day of the meeting. Instead of stewing in insecurities, I paddled the subject with a friend, walked around the ruins of astonishing history upon a large island, and found a friend in an elderly woman who had met the caretakers of a home and farm they had occupied on it in the early part of the 20th century.

Circumstances, a natural interest in history, and a fear of being exposed in a large crowd all conspired to place me inside the story.

Water follows the path of least resistance.

I will continue entering the story wherever I am, and delight in sharing it with others. There is an ongoing story unfurling all around you. An unfortunate tendency of our times is descent into like-minded tribes, hunkering down in perceived safety, and willful ignorance of the overarching story. Life becomes richer when we enter in, join the story, and share it.

We needn't discard cherished principles. As someone forever incapable of blending in with the cool kids, I've finally learned that our differences actually heighten the experience.

Act V

The wind of the storm fills our sails

37

Crossing the Rubicon — **40** — triggers soul-searching. Disentangling the rat's nest of existential questions is well-nigh impossible inside a chaotic, overly complex life.

Physical mess often flows from inward discombobulation. Clearing out the clutter always felt too complicated, so we nibbled at the edges. Ultimate inspiration and clarity came from an unlikely source: a dead Finnish immigrant.

Nearly impossible to comprehend, Eli Wirtanen passed away just 19 years before I was born. My, how times change.

Eli emigrated to the New World as a teenager in the late 1880s. At 34, he had enough money to purchase a 40-acre tract of land.

Densely forested and landlocked, there were no roads. Trails, such as the nearby Vermilion Trail, provided access to the outside world by foot or horseback.

Eli cut the trees and uprooted thousands of stumps by

hand and by horse. Nothing came easy. Handouts didn't exist. He dug his own well. (Remember my 4-foot hole?)

Wirtanen's farm survives to this day, preserved by a small group of volunteers, 40 miles north of Duluth.

The family and I spent a Sunday afternoon in late fall at the old farmstead, enjoying complete run of the place. Eli was a contemporary of Laura Ingalls Wilder, so it was easy for my kids to connect with him and his time. Racing between a dozen structures, spaced far apart to prevent a single fire from destroying everything, the children opened unlocked doors. Faces beamed in wonderment as they emerged from structures built from materials taken from the forest, calling across the land, "Come see what I've found!"

A fine day of unbridled play, we hurled the pigskin beneath towering Norway pines—sentinels through centuries.

It's a place where one may freely explore, coax imagination from its cave, and soak in quiet, understated beauty. Innovations of old are around every corner, such as the wooden gutter gracing the original sauna.

Opportunity for basking in unsanitized history, unshackled from rules or locked doors, is rare.

The simple lives and work ethic of pioneers draw me like a fly to honey. In this stage of the midlife crisis, the midpoint of my 40th year around the sun (eye of the storm), I redoubled efforts to simplify life and focus on what matters.

A resolve to dispose of burdensome collections materialized. Wirtanen, who lived in a sparse two-room cabin, would have found these objects baffling. Toted around for decades, they consumed valuable space and mental bandwidth. 25,000 baseball cards were an albatross. I poured thousands of hours and dollars into a collection of cardboard rectangles. As these accumulated, I hoarded animals in my bedroom. A hundred critters: eating, breathing, crapping, humping. Procreation on steroids.

The cards were no less toxic than ample bird droppings and seed hulls collecting between my sheets.

What distinguishes collecting from hoarding?

I received eight crisp $20 bills for them all, less than I had paid for a single card. Walking away from my "investment" felt incredible. The weight lifted.

Real treasure cannot be contained in totes.

These over-the-top accumulations were harmful. A steady flow of cash from delivering newspapers, coupled with little sense of responsibility or supervision, enabled a natural bent toward obsession. The paper route income from the age of 12, drawn from 10 hours of mostly pleasant work each week, dwarfed Eli's winter earnings in lumber camps. Excess money in the hands of a child, even adults, isn't necessarily beneficial. A little guidance, a saver's ethic, and a spirit of generosity are crucial for long-term success.

It was humbling to reflect upon how hard Eli worked to grub out such a basic existence. He traveled across the planet, saved tiny amounts of cash, and endured countless hardships prior to securing the land he'd work for 50 years. While never knowing the comforts of electricity or an automobile, he was self-sufficient and free.

Wirtanen helped me realize, in middle age, that I didn't want to spend the rest of my life beset by the goal of clearing out clutter. I just needed to do it. Heading into late fall, when others may have focused on income generation, I honed in on this lifelong quest. Essential to my wellbeing, there were emotional and spiritual dimensions to it. We cannot realize our full potential when our minds are overwhelmed by too many things.

Transformation of home and yard into a finely tuned economic engine was our goal. Stripping out the unessential… was essential.

Taking pictures of things, reflecting on the memories they represented, aided the process. Among the favorites, I bear the entire heap of papers and notes from favorite college and graduate school classes. Though stored and moved around for two decades, I never consulted them.

Did tens of thousands of dollars invested into higher education boil down to this stack of papers? Wisdom's accumulation? Casting them into the recycle bin was liberation.

Given how bewitching the baseball cards had been, it's ironic that I don't have a single photograph of a formerly impressive collection. My oldest card, and our home, were both built in 1910. What might I have done with all the time and energy that went into them?

Our home is now in its 113th year. My family is just the fourth to live here. We feel a responsibility to care for this place, while maximizing its potential for our family and others. Someday we'll pass it on to another family in a better condition than which we received.

When the newspaper called, desiring a story about Shawna and her home studio, it couldn't have come at a better time. What otherwise may have taken a month, or even a lifetime, was compressed into four days. Virtually all clutter was removed from the living space. Everything downstairs, stem to stern, and on up the steps through our upstairs hallway, was painted in creamy white. With such limited time, going with a single color sped things along nicely. The pressure of a high-profile news story helped us reach a lifelong goal, and the place looked amazing. We opened the home with nary a skeleton in our closets.

Several hours spent with a reporter and photographer produced a marvelous newspaper feature that consumed an entire page and a half.

The secret to maintaining a clean house is to actually have a clean house. One stray piece of paper stands out amidst order. Previously we'd get to 80% clean, only to discover that clutter breeds more clutter. This is a law of physics.

Like those rats, an outer manifestation of inner chaos...

Establishing order required saying yes to a few things;

no to many more. Hauling away an overabundance of potentially useful items created space for the people and things I most cherish, clearing the path forward.

Any hope for achieving our modest goals required an overhaul. Cutting out the objects I didn't love was the simplest place to start. A person—mind, body, soul—is a more complicated kettle of fish than a heap of stuff. The removal of these burdens is like pulling up an anchor, affording easier navigation of the river of life.

Later, feeling light and nimble, we'd apply these principles to our economic world. We were engaged in too many things in 2016. Beginnings are for broad brush strokes. Gradually, one whittles down to those few things they're best at, which bring the most value to the community. It's virtually impossible to discern these in advance. You've got to get in the ring and learn by doing.

Shawna made 100 paintings, carrying them into six exhibitions that year. She arrived as an artistic force from out-of-nowhere. This wasn't sustainable forever, but was essential at the outset. Eventually, after all this output of wildly varying styles and content, she produced a painting called Watering the Wallpaper. This successful experiment helped her focus on what became her unique style for the next several years. A girl is standing atop a hardwood floor, but her body reaches into the floral wallpaper with a matching dress (chameleon-like). She tips a watering can over a flower.

Somewhat similarly, my initial foray into farming had me caring for too many crops, while keeping chickens, and aggressively working toward branching out into pigs and bees. Major mayhem and stress in the following year proved beneficial in the long run. It forced me to shrink the operation down to minimum viability, right-sized for our family, and sustainable for the long run.

A tangled thicket of decisions lay ahead, requiring a level of perspicacity that did not come naturally. Ordering our physical world laid a solid foundation for developing clarity and a willingness to act upon the obvious.

38

The dog's death left a big hole.

Our kids started a puppy fund the next day. Reluctantly, I provided the jar to hold it.

Our income—more dribble than stream—was untouchable. The dream of an entire household bearing and contributing income required fruition.

Kicking things off, my daughter sold the five ducklings she reared herself and adored. As day-old cuties, they had been living bath toys. Thirty dollars entered the jar, a tough trade.

An extraordinary goal meant sacrifice. Our ten-year-olds embraced the challenge.

The kids scoured the basement in search of toys to sell. Money came in slowly, one bill at a time. George and Abe arrived on horseback from out of the way places.

We settled on obtaining a mini goldendoodle puppy from a reputable breeder. No more messing around with rescue dogs. This would be the family dog they'd remember forever.

The price tag was absurd. Just 25 of the $800 puppies would exceed that year's income. This was like buying a car.

When the jar crested a hundred bucks, an infection set in that became unstoppable. Each of us engaged cheerfully in a nearly impossible task, together, and shed unnecessary weight in a great decluttering. We edged toward our $800 goal, sometimes pennies at a time. Items large and small were hauled away.

I sold those burdensome collections hoarded since childhood. Addition through subtraction. They had become junk in boxes, bogging me down in the past, in the vain hope that their value might increase.

The entire family learned to prize what storage boxes cannot hold: friendship, shared experiences, spiritual growth, true love. These treasures increase in the lives of those who freely give them away.

I sold the lobster trap for a whopping $45. We picked it up at a junkyard in Nova Scotia for a buck during our honeymoon. Sentimental value transferred into 5% of a future dog.

We unloaded at least 500 pounds of stuff for cash, and still we didn't have enough for a three-pound golden puppy.

We brainstormed means of leveraging talents in family meetings around the dinner table. Our daughter started a small business on Etsy selling crafts and artwork. Another twenty went into the jar after raking leaves for neighbors.

Irresistible momentum spurred Shawna on to offer pet portraits. She quickly gained a commission. Everybody was fully invested.

Individual efforts became collective, as we cheered each other on in the relay race. Baton passed from one person to the next. We shared the strain. Most unexpectedly, the project brought us closer together over several months.

Against all odds, we reached our goal. The parents hadn't engineered success, making the experience sweeter. All four cylinders fired flawlessly in a household economy that performed better than I dared to hope.

Impregnable boundaries and limits, set by an inability to rush out and buy a new dog, were wonderful. Our contentious twins worked together and received adequate grieving time while waiting. These breakthroughs, among many intangibles, wouldn't have happened if I had whipped out the credit card in August. Instead, we were afforded a Christmas for the ages.

Voluntary simplicity is laudable. Involuntary simplicity is sublime. Many of our family's simplification efforts have fallen into this category. Oddly enough, involuntary simplicity is beautifully momentous. The price is acceptance. We can't be dragged into it kicking and screaming.

Soulless statistics placed us below the poverty line, but experiences like this reinforced and promoted abundance.

39

The metropolis needs surrounding rural areas, as a rubber tire requires a metal rim. Neither can thrive without the other. Viewing a pastoral landscape through a windshield, reducing it to pretty scenery, will not suffice.

As a city dweller, my wellbeing demands a regular inoculation of the country. That fall, after gathering all our hay into the barn, I journeyed out to procure a winter's worth of grass-fed beef and pork. The day's adventure nourished mind, body, and soul.

I visited seven entrepreneurs on the journey, most of whom were farmers, but I also dropped in on an artist.

Adam Swanson had recently moved from a sketchy neighborhood to a log cabin in the woods. The boys now have free run of the forest. His wife tends gardens, chickens, and goats.

A whimsical painting of diminutive gnomes amidst a flush of mushrooms, signed simply by, "Nana," hangs in a happy home.

Signs point to a family firmly rooted in land and community, no longer hanging in the balance. A sense of abundance and wellbeing hangs in the air. Creative overflow seems all but assured for the foreseeable future.

Ironically, after peppering Adam with intrusive questions about finances flying in from disparate sources and inviting myself to a tour of his log home, I was bereft of courage when bowels notified brain of an impending evacuation. Camping out in the bathroom of a near-stranger for an extended period felt too indiscreet.

Big mistake.

The next twenty minutes found me barreling down the road, increasingly desperate. My brain was so consumed by an urgent need to control that final inch of digestive tract that all executive functioning ceased. Panic reached its apogee as I entered Christopher's driveway.

He was away at his day job, but had provided instructions for collecting a gallon of maple syrup. As if bursting forth from a cannon, I launch into the deciduous forest. 50 feet in, within sight of the clearing, I crouched. Apparently overwhelmed by ecstatic relief, I lost track of time and space. After re-entering my body, I was horrified to discover a truck in the driveway. The considerable noise of an aging pickup creeping up a lengthy gravel avenue had eluded my senses. How was this possible??? What are the odds that he'd pull in, unscheduled during work hours, at this precise moment?

Sheepishly, I pulled up my trousers and walked around to the garage where he waited discreetly out of sight, handed him a check without the usual pleasantries, and got the heck out of there.

I sourced all of our family's maple syrup from him for the first two years of his little business. We stumbled across his sign along Highway 4 on our way to berry-picking a year after he purchased the land. I noted fascinating improvements with each visit. The oaks cut down to build his own driveway were milled into usable lumber, dried inside a homemade solar kiln, and pieced back together into a house that slowly materialized.

Engaged and living alone in a tiny garage when I met him, his bride embraced the challenge of joining him in the small space. Evidence of bootstrap frugality abounded at every turn. Their plan was to enjoy the garage for at least another year, incurring minimal debt, and completing the house themselves little by little with cash on hand. How can anyone not wish success for such salt of the earth?

Butt, I haven't been back since that chilly day in 2016. Crap. I have missed much. A clutch of kids are probably running around the finished house right now. Our maple syrup, purchased at the grocery store these days, costs a few dollars more. More than any savings from buying in bulk, I've missed small observations of their lives, those moments spent peering into the very foundation of a family and legacy.

I thought of them with every splash of maple syrup atop my wife's scratch-made pancakes, telling the kids about where it was painstakingly made, came up through the trees (drawn from the land itself) and was carefully evaporated down to perfection at a 40:1 ratio. These moments are an opportunity to pray for the people and families who invest so much of themselves into the little bits of sweetness added to my home and sense of place. Gratitude is inescapable.

Christopher, I'm sorry I left my DNA in your woods. Perhaps you'll come across this obscure book and have a good chuckle. Might our relationship resume? I'll stop in annually to marvel at your skills, enjoy the fruit of your land, and promise to keep my Fruit of the Looms firmly affixed to hips and out of sight.

Relationships are messy. The price of humanity...

Next, feeling lighter, I dropped in on Catherine. The sight of her newly completed home, located conveniently beside her CSA farm, was stunning. If you recall, she slept alone in a small bedroom at the rear of an outbuilding when I initially dropped in on her.

231

Ten years into her farming odyssey, she and Elden finally completed a beautiful home on the property. On the heels of such sacrifice, it brought me immense joy to tour their unique dwelling.

Rather than expecting farmers to live a hands-to-mouth existence, we should find pleasure in seeing those who feed us being nourished themselves.

The view through Catherine's floor-to-ceiling windows, looking south across her fields, is the very picture of agrarian serenity. I'm left with abiding gladness over their successful collusion in fortitude in building a life together that clearly suits them.

This feeling of joy in seeing real lives steadily improving is impossible to experience when food and entertainment are metaphorically beamed to you from a distant mothership, somewhere out there, but who really knows where…

Just beyond Catherine's fields, clearly visible before the woods, sit Adam Kemp's strawberry fields. Now on the cusp of winter, his strawberries are liberally added to my hot cereal. The frozen red berries impart summer's deliciousness, and memories of a fine hour of picking right up to the moment of a thunderstorm's arrival. With each individual berry tossed into the pot, and ultimately into my mouth, I feel profound satisfaction and appreciation for the soil and people that produced these bombs of sweetness.

Bonafide culture that nourishes a community includes art AND agriculture. A populace that cannot, or will not, feed and entertain itself is hardly worthy of being called a community. With so many among us lacking connection to land, neighbor, and creative overflow, cohesion fails. The fabric of local lore is woven in large measure by artists and storytellers.

Those who feed and entertain us are worthy of double honor. Purveyors of beauty and good cheer must live joyous lives themselves, far beyond the clutches of poverty, for culture to thrive. This must be our desire, and indeed our joy.

I previously identified myself beneath a certain brand of politics. Spending time with these beautiful people, and many more who cannot be contained within this humble volume, nudged me to skew human instead. Meaningful relationships are more important than being right about individual issues.

Instead of succumbing to a winner-take-all system, conservatives and liberals need one another. The simple appreciation of neighbors, grasping our common humanity and goals, could liberate us from the tyranny of an unhealthy national obsession over politics. It's difficult to be angry with someone over political differences after coming to love them, even though they are so very different. Life becomes more satisfying, interesting, and enjoyable. Wealth is abundant. Renewable.

Resting in satisfaction and enjoyment of your neighbor's surplus is a happier place than conspiracy theories and bitterness. Must we argue about hot-button issues outside our control? Can't we just enjoy the strawberries?

40

Inexplicably, I re-enlisted. All that fumbling around—a thousand bucks in exchange for chaos—paid off.

It helped me understand specific areas of weakness. Inexperience could be put into harness through time-tested systems. Also, the Schedule F I included with my taxes so reluctantly (needing every dollar to maximize the Earned Income Credit) made us eligible for a $10,000 USDA loan.

Even with my middling efforts, the Ag rep saw promise in the high price per pound for chickens, and in the notion of bio-intensively farming unused lawns so profitably per square foot. Money in hand, my first $900 went into an online course called Profitable Urban Farming. Rather than re-invent the wheel, it was time to learn from someone else's mistakes. A guy has only so many crushing defeats inside him. If this season ended like the last one, I'd probably quit.

The farm occupied a seventh of an acre. Incredibly, this

was still too large for my skill level. My farm plan had me planting and harvesting 200 beds throughout a 30-week season. The volume of decisions required for the ambitious blueprint that had me shooting for a $14,000 profit was overwhelming. Paralysis by analysis was a distinct possibility.

The dizzying array of choices posed to a farmer every single day was by far the biggest shocker about going into this line of work. Educated guesses, or even coin flips, will make do sometimes. More often than not, hundreds of decisions are arrived at after painstaking thought, exhaustive research, and consultation with those who have gone before.

What type of irrigation should I use? Which products should be purchased to support this choice? How should I carve up the city lot to yield the maximum number of garden beds?

After much deliberation, informed by mistakes and inefficiencies from the prior season, I settled on a standard bed size of 30 inches wide by 25 feet long. Several hours spent with graph paper, pencil, and ruler, showed I could cram 60 of these beds into the space. I'd turn these over several times throughout the season. 200 individual crop cycles and harvests within 60 beds worked intensively from spring to fall.

The online course's spreadsheet provided a starting point. It contained an astonishing amount of data that I didn't have to discover on my own: specific crops, pricing, weekly sales goals by crop throughout a 30-week season, days to maturity from seed, average yield per bed for each crop, and so much more. The complexity only begins with what to plant and when to plant it. This style of farming requires far more brain power and planning than civilians will ever understand.

With all these choices directed at an amateur, individual failures were inevitable, but I was as prepared as I'd ever be after securing financing, knowledge, and professional equipment. I was also granted a booth at the Duluth Farmer's Market, the most desirable option in town.

But, as the philosopher in Mike Tyson said, "Everybody has a plan until they get punched in the face."

Powerful blows landed in quick succession.

I had much of the land prepared in April, earlier than I ever thought possible. Black tarps rapidly heated the soil on sunny days, so I planted my first low tunnels (clear plastic supported by metal conduit pipes bent into hoops at the exact width of two beds and reaching about three feet in height to form inexpensive structures similar to a greenhouse).

After installing several of these over newly planted beds, the landowner suddenly realized the ramifications of an impending balloon payment on the property in tandem with extensive repairs. Wisdom called out to sell it. Buttoned-up realtor advised shutting down the farm.

Crap!

To the church's credit, they insisted I remain as long as possible, but in a hot housing market, the home sold immediately. With the sale pending, I received conflicting information. Hopes soared after learning I could farm out the season, only to have them dashed upon hearing that the farm would vanish after the sale. Back and forth we'd go.

I kept pressing on.

Then came a shattering detonation. A single day in May, perfect for working outside, became the most stressful of my life. All of the following went down within a span of 15 hours:

1. With a week of rain in the forecast, I was determined to complete most of the field work. Though the property's sale was imminent, hints were dropped that I might finish out the season after all. At the very moment of reaching down to fire up the tiller to form more garden beds, that fancy iPhone jumped around inside my bib pocket. The buyers

pulled the plug on the farm. I needed to vacate the property. Immediately. What?????

2. Two hours later, our only vehicle blew its engine. EPIC DISASTER! My only thought upon getting the call from my wife, crying hysterically along the side of the road, was, "Of course." Everything was going wrong: expensive appliances, land up in smoke, and now the family car. One more thing for the pile. With a quote that came to $5600, and a warning that it might cost more, an ask of a million dollars couldn't have been more shocking or irrelevant. Crush the car. This was roughly our combined income earned by this date in mid-May 2017, and we weren't on Food Stamps (goodness, that sure would have helped).

3. Shawna's new laptop, a necessity for her art business, was flooded with water.

And we thought a breakdown of the dehumidifier a couple days prior was a big deal...

This was beyond any and all comprehension. If I could have plotted out a timeline for my life, much like those 200 garden beds, and planned for all this to land in the worst possible season of life (let alone on a single day), this was it. We were already up against the ropes.

It's impossible to exaggerate this experience's value. We came to understand in our core, viscerally, that everything is beyond the bounds of our control. As problems grew gargantuan, well beyond any means of extrication, we learned to do what little we could and wait for solutions to present themselves. The choreography was too perfect to ascribe to random chance. Rather than fight it, we learned to trust. My faith deepened while accepting that these setbacks had been ordained to wallop us all at once.

Ultimately, we are not what we own or what we do.

Feeling defeated, we got up the next day and did what was in front of us. There were no solutions, or even considering them.

I put the finishing touches on an interior paint job, an entire home, netting us a couple thousand dollars. Mindless work, coupled with the knowledge of a payday, was a gift.

Boom. The next month of bare expenses was covered.

Shawna poured her energy into painting increasingly complex works of art. After the kids got on the bus, 45 minutes after the water fiasco, she returned to a piece called Lost At Sea. With a giant wave breaking over a boy blending in with the wall as he serenely went about his reading, it seemed oddly fitting. So much water!

We slowly came to terms with a reality that might not have us owning a car or land to farm that year. Life is more than such externalities. We'd still be a family without them. I contemplated riding the bus to the farmers market, lugging coolers three blocks up the hill across the last stretch on foot. What an experience that would have been!

The unfurling disaster left us awash in kindness. Friends and family stepped in to help, cheerfully, and without being asked. My wife's parents loaned us their regular car, temporarily turning a 1949 Mercury hotrod (usually garaged) into their own work vehicle. Shawna's brother drove six hours roundtrip, trailering the car back to the Twin Cities, where he plugged away at installing an affordable used engine for weeks. We didn't even know he was coming until he arrived.

We waited for a solution to come to us, and it did.

Learning to work on a hybrid, he carefully unplugged and tweezed apart the entire front end of the car. With hoses dangling uselessly into a shocking chasm, a tangle of plastic and metal, it looked like a T-Rex had taken out a large bite. Through an abundance of perseverance and patience, he put Humpty Dumpty back together again, only to discover that the transmission was wrecked. Bryan mined the same junkyard for a tranny and tore everything apart all over again, devoting two months of spare time to learning how the puzzle pieces worked together.

When the parents inevitably needed their car back, other friends—some barely more than acquaintances—cheerfully volunteered old trucks without being asked. I fit right in at the farmers market and supply store in these pickups. It felt good to roll up in a rig adequate for hauling a thousand pounds of chicken feed.

Shawna's computer came through the crisis too. The solution was simple. Leave it off, turn it upside down to dry for two days, and walk away. Much like everything else, it paid off to wait. Either it would work again or it wouldn't.

The same thing applied to the land. Multiple realtors and intermediaries had confused things. When I met the buyers in person, they couldn't have been more delightful. The prospect of having a serious gardener on site excited them. I provided yummy produce each week, made improvements to the soil, and would put it all into grass upon leaving. It was a win-win for everyone. They had bigger fish to fry inside the fixer-upper.

I could never repay these people, far too many to list, for their many kindnesses. Even if this were possible, it would only cheapen the gifts they offered. This is grace. Totally undeserved; a marvel to bask in.

The darkness of difficult circumstances makes the light glorious, a sort of beatific vision. Gratitude for these offerings— love and compassion in action—remains with me forever. I'll never be the same.

My foray in the farmers market exceeded expectations. The Saturday before Memorial Day weekend, I sold $400 in microgreens and a few bunches of radishes. Arriving on a 39-degree and depressingly damp day, fearing a week of work would rot as compost, I stood behind my booth swaddled in thick wool from head to toe, and sold out. Week after week went by like that, as I hustled to have every visitor to the market taste microgreens. Because of the land crisis, I had thrown nearly everything into growing an indoor crop at a place I controlled. Amazingly, they were a massive hit. Momentum grew from there as the weather improved, I gained confidence, and customers brought their friends.

41

Kneeling in a prayerful position of surrender, I jammed row after row of tiny transplants into the ground. As the sun set on a 17-hour workday in early June, we were desperate for these plants to produce. While begging protection for hundreds of seedlings, there was satisfaction in this posture of complete dependence. Kinship with men and women of the soil across the ages who similarly placed knees in direct contact with the soil manifested. For us, prayer wasn't intellectual or rote. Crying out through the fog of mystery and doubt was survival, not lip service.

Bleakness, thick and pervasive, was beyond comprehension. All we could do was huddle together and put one foot forward at a time. Baby steps into the unknown.

Dwelling on the darkness of our plight was unthinkable. It was time to simply do.

So, I did.

Trusted.

Waited.

Fully submitted to forces beyond control.

There was no guaranteed income, such as unemployment pay or food stamps. Our only vehicle blew an engine and transmission. We had faced the loss of what I assumed was the farm's economic engine. Appliances were crumbling into dust. Kids were cranky. The list went on.

The basic elements of our lives melted down in a crucible. I sensed purpose behind the trials, but it was shrouded in mystery. Something new was being forged. Though our days were marked by an unsustainable crush of busyness and gastrointestinal distress, HOPE was in the air. Even then, I could see these struggles were necessary for long-term success. Now, with hindsight's clarity, I'm thankful for them. There were lasting benefits beyond my limited understanding, but here are two life-changing impacts that spring to mind:

1. We experienced community and family in a manner hitherto unknown.
2. At least five years of wisdom were distilled into eight weeks. The endurance of massive blows is better in the long run than death by a thousand cuts.

The trials of this period were heavier than I could have shouldered on my own, so people came out of the woodwork to lend a helping hand. Learning to receive their gifts, experiencing tangible blessings, was wonderful. Not wanting our predicament to burden others, I didn't reach out for help. Inexplicably, we were never left wanting for a vehicle. When Mike needed his truck back, for example, Brandon called out of the blue to offer his. This is extraordinarily consequential when the complete sum of your work must be delivered to two farmers markets each week, restaurants, and grocery stores. My father-in-law built the farm's walk-in cooler unassisted.

I could rattle off dozens of indispensable kindnesses.

Having grown up in an atmosphere of poverty, always penny-pinching, generosity has never come naturally. Being on the receiving end, sensing how even the smallest gifts kept us back from the edge of insanity and ruin, informs a lifetime's growth. Equally beneficial, are a handful of moments when kindness was lacking. What if, for example, a cheerful person had emerged from a nearby home with a plate of cookies while I waited forlornly for the tow truck in plain sight? Surely I can bring simple compassionate neighborliness to a stranger in similar circumstances.

The young man who screamed, "Faggot!" from the window of a passing car at the guy on a bicycle wearing bib overalls and holding a pitchfork like a triton was also instructive.

By the time we pressed our car back into service, I had discovered that I didn't enjoy schlepping around town for a multi-locational farm. I'd rather grow what I can right here at home, accepting the limitations for what they are. This was such a valuable lesson. With no work/life balance, quality time with the family disappeared as I hustled for survival. My kids were already 12 years old. Something had to give. I resolved to prune the farm of everything unessential.

The chickens were an obvious place to begin. We raised one more batch of birds that summer, just to prove to ourselves we could do it. With a profit amounting to $8 per chicken, we concluded one needs to live on-site for this to make sense. After correcting for a couple mistakes, we were confident that future batches would top out at $10 per head. With 95 birds brought to butcher, basic math shows this isn't worth the stress of eight weeks of effort, or driving back and forth to the pasture. Weaving the simple daily chores into a routine as part of a traditional farm, while simultaneously reaping the fertilizing benefits of all that free nitrogen from amazing bird crap, is another story altogether. But it wasn't my reality. Rather than bemoan my presence outside of that context, I accepted it. We would have expanded the operation if desperate times hadn't been forced upon us.

Finishing out the process was great fun. The consistent collision of beauty and struggle became a source of humor and awe. Arriving at 5 am one morning, I was spellbound by an approaching storm. A rainbow, like the Bifrost in appearance, cleaved the sky between violence and peace. Moments after pausing to appreciate unfurling drama, the thunderstorm enveloped me in rain, hail, and dangerous lightning. I laughed hysterically while dragging the chicken tractor onto fresh grass and scrambled to feed and water everyone before racing home.

The project was also a lesson on functioning in partnership. Life is never split down the middle 50/50 between willing partners, as if Mommy perfectly divided the cake. Perhaps this resonates so strongly because I raise twins, but was an only child myself. Fairness is always in the background. This discovery has become a hobby horse that has strengthened our marriage, so please allow a small indulgence here.

In any partnership—business, marriage, friendship—the workload shouldered by each participant is always fluctuating, never static. The key element is trust, an understanding that both are equally committed to the success of the whole. Actual work accomplished by each party swings back and forth, like a pendulum, in the range of a 40/60% split in terms of exerted effort. The ideal cleaving of exact portions occurs only briefly as the pendulum swings in an organic overflow of individual giftedness and capacity at each moment in time.

This dream of raising pastured meat was impossible without a partner. We were even on the cusp of expanding and branching out into pigs and sheep in other locations. My context as a city-dweller restricts this interest, but it was worth pursuing with Matt's help.

The two of us are opposites in many ways. Our strengths complemented one another's weaknesses. Almost impossible to comprehend now, Matt worked in the fashion industry. I chuckled to think of him all gussied up like a pretty boy for his main gig that utilized considerable skills in design, store layout, and other qualities. His bent toward design and planning runs rings around me.

Our second year as chicken wranglers was a successful trial run accomplished with minimal risk. When the appointed time arrived (maturity just eight weeks after hatching!) they were all loaded into an old van received in a trade for vegetables. The one-hour drive to the processor was a keep-the-windows down affair. Pine-scented air fresheners wouldn't have touched the stink. That powerful odor, on the drive home as the birds fulfilled their purpose, burned a sense of satisfaction into us I suspect will linger on forever. Climbing back onto this horse, and then quitting after moderate success, was a fabulous way to bring the partnership toward dissolution.

Total sales came in at $1792 vs $1000 in expenses, some of which were one-time costs. We were confident that small tweaks could have raised the profit by another 25% going forward. It takes practice to raise quick-growing chickens at scale.

But I didn't enjoy driving eight miles each way to perform 20 minutes of work, and then obsess all night long about whether I had latched the gate. Removing two months of daily chicken-obsession would free up an immense amount of spare capacity. For the sake of a well-rounded family life, I honed in on enterprises that paid most efficiently.

I'm forever grateful to have ventured this far down the rabbit hole, however. I am left with a memory and friendship impossible to achieve by reading books, or pining after an unrealistic future utopia as a gentleman farmer. Moving through the process, experiencing all the highs and lows, was incredibly valuable.

Back to the partnership, I guarantee that one of us put in 55% of the work. I handled all the sales, incurring logistical headaches. The consistent flow of customers to my back alley garage had me consider the possibility that my elderly neighbors may have assumed I was operating a meth lab. Matt, on the other hand, built the brooder in his garage this time, where the chickens spent their first three weeks. Does it really matter who put in slightly more effort?

When Matt had to step away for business trips, I filled in the gaps. On a couple occasions, overwhelmed by demands imposed by the veggie farm and twice-weekly farmers markets, I put out the SOS for him to shoulder my share of the morning moves and feedings. Neither of us complained. Reality required each of us to step beyond that mythical 50% for the sake of the enterprise's overall success.

Objectively speaking, bean-counting is just plain stupid. If one of us worked 10% harder, perhaps they were entitled to an additional $79.20 of the profit. Is that paltry amount worthy of all the stress, controversy, and mental gymnastics? Similar amounts are at play in all areas of life, including friendships and marriage. Nothing is ever equal.

As it turned out, Matt let me keep all the money. He took the equipment. I think I got the better deal. I also feel like I married up, that my neighbors give me more value than I give them, and so forth.

Shawna has a similar mindset within our marriage. Our family went through the fire, and this came on the back of years of income-stress. Anxiety reached critical levels as stress and a back-breaking workload mounted. If either of us had fallen into bean-counting, well, I don't know. Marriages have imploded for lesser reasons.

Rather than being a source of stress, our partnership in life is a refuge. A place of calm. We're both committed. This doesn't mean the load is ever pulled equally. We rest in absolute trust and confidence in one another, desiring only the best for each of our endeavors and our family. The household economy—

the family's overall wellbeing—takes priority over individual ambitions.

I've always been a pseudo-loner, ever on the outside looking in. The experience of community and family in new and deeper ways was marvelous. Often recited at weddings, the following text is a familiar one. It was written nearly two thousand years ago to a ragged group of people struggling to live out their faith, and were failing at the most basic levels. I came to understand these words viscerally, deep down in my core.

Love is patient, love is kind. It does not envy, it does not boast, it is not proud. It does not dishonor others, it is not self-seeking, it is not easily angered, it keeps no record of wrongs. Love does not delight in evil but rejoices with the truth. It always protects, always trusts, always hopes, always perseveres.

Finally, on to the second easily identifiable purpose, a half-decade of farming wisdom was shoehorned into eight weeks of hard knocks. Many middling farmers scratch by good enough to give it one more shot the following year, finding themselves mired in poverty for decades. Multiple crises stripped us of the luxury of a slow death. In just two months, Tiny Farm Duluth's future course was set. I never could have arrived at our unique and enviable niche under my own designs. It would have taken me far too long.

While the new owners of my farm's main plot cheerfully allowed me full reign of their large yard throughout the season, the stress of the process had set me back. The joy in being there had been sucked away. Developing a relationship with them helped a ton, but I needed to garden my own land and uncover joy in soil's improvement without worry of losing it later. My work in and upon their dirt had been back-breaking while maneuvering truckloads of compost and coming to understand its idiosyncrasies. I couldn't deal with the notion of it all being put into grass and walking away. Some people can do this effectively by not forming an emotional attachment, but my style demands a personal connection with everything I touch.

"It's not personal. It's only business," doesn't apply to me.

Through the endurance of eight weeks of hell, I resolved to squeeze the entire farm onto my own property, and thus compress the gardening space down from 7,000 square feet to 625. This made perfect sense, because it aligned a key economic engine to our values. My goal, from the very moment of being sacked three years prior, was for 100% of income to emanate from our home.

Microgreens were the cream that rose to the top. By this point, through twice-weekly harvests, I had already experienced 20 iterations of the crop. Knowledge and understanding came quickly through so many successes and failures. Fear of losing our home applied motivation.

The dust settled.

42

The farm plot produced handsomely, even as my heart moved on. While devoting myself to transforming our backyard into the market garden of the future, numerous crops came into harvest at the more distant site.

The farmers market was a cash cow, jamming $1000 into my pocket every week across two market days. With a market booth bursting with greens, I was practically the only option for a crowd desperate for fresh produce in Spring. The high-water mark came in July, notching $1300 on a Saturday. Too busy to trifle with deposits, I had cash coming out of my ears. My body was breaking down as I filled every available tote and cooler with umpteen options. I prepped for that blowout market until 3 am, finishing with a salad mix, of which I sold just $65 worth because every other farmer had lettuce by that time. Like most rookies, I needed to lean the operation down and concentrate resources on cash crops.

The 80/20 rule, ruthlessly employed, guided me into the future. If 20% of the crops produced 80% of the income, why not focus 100% on them? Limited space, time, and ability channeled me into a niche where I was capable of long-term success. Rather than fight personal and environmental limitations, I embraced them.

The problem became the solution.

Desperate for multiple market streams, I approached a handful of grocery stores. Normal circumstances would have dictated waiting another year, but the need to feed my family was real. My pitch to produce managers was simple. "I sell 150 of these clamshells every week…"

As surplus field crops piled up, restaurants welcomed me into their kitchens. When the USDA rep came out to audit their investment in August, the farm was in its glory. The tiny footprint had already produced $14,000, with more to come. Their first loan to an urban farm, the results impressed them.

I snapped a photo to mark the occasion. Beets, basil, carrots, and lettuce thrived in all stages, as succession planting continued after each crop came out. Grandma's Magic Beans added a lovely backdrop, soaring eight feet into the sky along the homeowner's rear fence. Deep purple on the vine, they turn green when cooked. A hundred years of family stewardship placed these seeds into my hands, easily dried and planted year after year. They are fantastic, but picking them was time-consuming. Managing all this was too much.

It became essential to double down on the 80/20 rule, Pareto's Law. Those early days of appearing so capable with an array of crops and gorgeous photos on Instagram are beguiling, as was walking into a restaurant as a tour de force with dozens of options. My farm's stable predictability sometimes disappoints inquiring chefs these days: no edible flowers, rare experimentation or new offerings, the same bread and butter options 52 weeks a year.

In choosing to settle in at a marathon's pace, rather than a sprint, personal limitations become success's guarantor.

That said, the satisfaction of having grown so many crops lingers. I proved to myself that I can do it. In the end, I ceded this work to capable farmers with better resources. I'm not as young as that Wrenshall gang was when they cut their teeth. Being at a different stage of life, in my 40s and tethered to the city, I learned to appreciate the reality that I'll never be as good a farmer as they are. However, I can nerd out with them on the nitty gritty, which brings me joy.

At the farmers market, many crops arrive in super-abundance all at once. When everybody brings in truckloads of similarity, items become commoditized, facilitating a race to the bottom in prices. My booth was next to big Mike, an older fella, now retired. His prices hadn't budged in 20 years. The elderly woman shaking her head at my booth while scoffing at a $4 bag of Red Russian Kale, beautiful and tender in its baby stage, was instructive.

"I pay a dollar for my kale."

Returning home, I entered sales in a spreadsheet, inputting totals like $9, $45, $65, $19, and then $525 for the microgreens. This wasn't a complicated decision, but I had to walk through it. I arrived at the solution of microgreens over that challenging two-month period, and never could have contemplated such a thing beforehand. The outcome wasn't foreseeable.

Struggle was necessary for arriving. When monumental problems dwarf your capabilities, prioritize doing over thinking. Analytical reasoning inside the labyrinth is impossible. The path becomes obvious as we move forward.

A crisis—walked through instead of squandered through avoidance or self-pity—produces major returns in the long run. Sitting in the problem for an extended period has a way of presenting its own unavoidable solution. This approach of arriving at solutions, instead of imposing them, eases stress. Happily, it also seems to yield better results.

43

After squeezing everything into our home and lawn, I limited field crops to the barest of minimums for the sake of an enticing market booth. A colorful, three-foot pile of radishes lured shoppers over, providing an opportunity for sampling pea shoots. These are the baby pea plant themselves. Harvested young and tender, they're like a sweet pea salad. Juicy and delicious, they are the gateway into microgreens.

Our main outdoor crop was a premium baby lettuce mix, to which I added surplus microgreens and edible flowers. A small sign sat atop my booth for three years, alerting eaters to grocers stocking the micros. Thousands of individuals became acquainted with our products in this way. One can't help but slowly acquire serious year-round customers after eaters finally see family members and children become excited about salads and sandwiches. Many of these same people became fans of Shawna's artwork as well, through exposure to a crate of rotating prints. A stack of my books also rested on the table; the three-legged stool materialized, however humble.

Work was manageable again. Instead of being deluged by the demands of 60 garden beds, I obsessed about seven. Field work took place during mornings and evenings (instead of under a blasting sun). At the sound of, "Dinner's ready," a satisfying saunter carried me back to the family, where I was now much more present. Still far from perfect, I had enough freedom to mountain bike with my son once or twice every week. That previous summer, in 2017, we didn't even go one time! This was a major victory, even as my farmers market booth diminished from its former glory. I shifted from the hot, happening vendor bringing new things every week to boring and predictable.

Shrinking down to minimum viability required humility. Instead of the farm crowding out life, we let life encroach upon the farm.

When the kids wanted that trampoline, I sacrificed two more garden beds. Due to shade issues, they had only reached peak production at the height of summer anyway, but this loss was enough to knock me out of the market. A photo, snapped by my daughter, depicts this intermingling of family and business that previously eluded me. In the frame, she's hoisting some rare moth like a falconer. Behind this rare beauty rests the chaos of 10 X 20-inch microgreen trays drying atop every available chair after being dipped in sanitizing solution, lettuce in stages ranging from germination to maturity, and that dang trampoline that quickly faded into the background.

I was no longer capable of producing enough crops for an interesting market booth. The problem became the solution. Two years of a diminutive market space forced the inevitable conclusion that it wasn't worth time's sacrifice. My serious customers had already migrated toward obtaining microgreens at the Whole Foods Co-op, and their novelty had worn off among the usual crowd. Moving to a wholesale operation would free up

10 - 12 hours every week from May to October, otherwise known as the most beautiful time of year.

It was incredibly difficult to cut out the market. Knowing it was necessary, I burned this bridge by selling all my market gardening equipment (precision seeder, hoops for low tunnels, and much more) in the fall of 2019. This drastic action was necessary for following through with basic common sense. Though I came to a similar conclusion the previous season, I lingered on a year longer than necessary.

Now I'd have time for such extravagances as the ongoing quest to hike the entire Superior Hiking Trail with my son. Having space for things like this is priceless. After all, our crowded nest won't stay that way for long.

The arrangement is imperfect. I've cut the farm down to the bone, testing the limits of sanity. We have four regular products, all microgreens. As if this wasn't enough, I pruned off an under-performing grocery store during the pandemic to direct resources at the voracious demand of Co-op customers during the pandemic (for whom nutritional health became a clear priority).

Thankfully, as I have shrunk, Shawna's reach has grown. Our incomes have essentially matched, bringing a greater sense of security and abundance. She sold a $4,000 painting last summer (2022) as my sales experienced a cyclical dip, more than making up the difference.

We've been in humble territory at around $30K net profit each year, but we're on the upswing. It seems ironic that our income hasn't budged much, but that's only because I've relentlessly right-sized the farm to the intersection of my skill level and family's wholistic needs, while simultaneously investing in the future.

44

"I'm so tired of saying no to my kids when they want ice cream."

My neighbor's reply sent me into a tailspin.

"We never say no to ice cream…"

WHAT????

I retreated to The Pigeon. Described in my last book, the abandoned shack is my equivalent to Superman's ice palace. Semi-annual journeys here, deep in the boreal forest along the 48th parallel, aren't merely opportunities to recharge. It's a pilgrimage. Miles of travel through several feet of snow peels away layers. Body, mind, and soul succumb to harness and work together. Finally, usually after dark, we arrive. Removing skis and burdens from our backs, we descend into the cabin from atop a winter's collected output of moisture. Frozen eyelashes and feet thaw beside a roaring fire. Sleep is never a problem on that first night.

But this time it was. I wrestled with God like Jacob, twisting and turning atop my creaky bunk for eight hours. I came for peace, but felt only confusion. Time stood still throughout a dark night of the soul. Big changes were necessary. I was weary of working so hard, emotionally and physically, and having so little to show for it. Maybe I should just shut the farm down and get a job. It felt like a decision that would ripple down through the decades, and yet, this wasn't my identity.

For the first time in a quarter-century, I had hauled in the perfect book. The choice of reads is a weighty decision. When I was young and dumb, unable to decide on just one, I'd lug a small library in a giant backpack. Extra weight destroys you in all that powder. Falling down in it, up to your neck, and failing to roll back atop your skis while bearing such a burden, cures a guy of such stupidity. So, the pressure is on to stow away a single great read.

Journeying out to relieve oneself in the darkness is magical. Stars sparkle at maximum brilliance, with no hint of light pollution or even the suggestion that a city might exist anywhere. A gentle wind whispers through the treetops as smoke silently twists from the chimney on a conveyor belt to heaven. Turning back to the cabin, the warmest illumination imaginable trickles out the windows, icicles aglow from a half-dozen candles, beckoning you in to the most comfortable silence of your life. Occasional pops of wood igniting in the stove, and a gentle hiss of snow melting for drinking water, add subtle punctuations. This place is made for immersion: friendships, conversation, faith, wilderness, and reading. In peace...

As the other men snored, I entered the pages like the boy

in The NeverEnding Story. In granting perspective, they calmed the turbulence, carried me away in adventure, and opened my heart. The closeness of the family at the heart of the story was awe-inspiring. Though they had passed through the worst experience of their lives, they clung to one another. A hole in my heart emerged as I advanced through the pages, a loneliness rooted within a history as an only child in adversity. The bond between the brother and sister had me longing for a similar connection, often so elusive, in my own children. This book, Leif Enger's Peace Like a River, flooded into my life when I most needed it.

The story didn't answer a single question about an impossible vocational situation. It rehydrated a shriveled heart, affecting me on an emotional level that I hadn't expected while dealing with much bigger issues than whatever income my little farm threw off: identity, faith, family, relationships, loss, and so much more. It put my struggle into perspective. Closing the business wasn't the worst thing that could happen.

So, in March 2019, I chose door number two.

A job coach joined the team. He jazzed up my resume and urged use of a more traditional email address than eddygilmorehasleftthebuilding@theyayhoo. Over the course of the next year, I went hard after three jobs. I was compelling enough to gain interviews, but was too much of a wild card versus individuals with relevant experience.

I fantasized about rejoining the workforce at a salary of $50k, and treating my kids to ice cream now and again. Even though I became more valuable after learning to build a business and endure, it was deflating to discover I wouldn't come close to that figure.

The inability to command enough value to even match the paltry income of my last job was disheartening. A half-decade of trials had made me a far more resilient, valuable, and resourceful asset. Furthermore, if any job existed for me, the oddball email address wouldn't scare the right employer away. They'd be looking for a nontraditional hire.

When the pandemic hit and millions lost their jobs, I was thankful to not be among them.

I received a daily dose of depression in my inbox for two years from a world hellbent on pigeonholing me into unsuitable work. The promise of low-wage, soul-sucking work for the rest of my life nearly reeled me in. It wasn't personal. Just business...

In early 2021 while writing this very chapter, I finally unsubscribed from that email list. That last subject line read, "Dollar Store retail clerk and 16 other jobs..." Remaining on the path required encountering these roadblocks, reminders of a world for which I was ill-equipped.

Writing this book gave me the courage to sink permanent foundations. Concurrently, we added a large sunroom onto the south-facing rear of our home, Tiny Farm Duluth's final destination. The cost was staggering, requiring two years of gross sales. Committing after years of wavering was like reaching solid ground, stretching out and resting in the sun, after an arduous trek through a swamp. I'm no longer dithering over what to do with my life.

The freedom of committing is incredible.

This investment's shocking reality had triggered that crisis at The Pigeon two years earlier, after which I quashed a similar plan. The numbers didn't justify the risk. Increasing demand for microgreens during the pandemic had grown to a point where we needed to either take this leap or step into something else. The new space would bring my crop into maximum sunlight, while providing a professional environment I could delight in.

It wasn't the numbers that ultimately gave me the ability to rest in this choice. That moment arrived right here in chapter 44. Though I had penned a newspaper column and book prior to this, writing hadn't penetrated into daily life. I am quite good at growing microgreens, because I do it over and over again. Wash. Rinse. Repeat. In contrast to a potato farmer who may have grown a handful of annual crops by this stage of the game, I've experienced hundreds of weekly crop cycles. Learning by doing, constant iteration, is the way into mastery. I would never come close to writing my best work without incorporating a similar habit into daily life, and that's exactly what has happened.

Did I pull myself up by my own bootstraps and will this into existence? In part, perhaps, but it feels more like circumstances channeled me into this lifestyle. I don't believe I could have thought my way into this sweet spot by myself. Providence seems to have guided forward movement. The great labor of telling this story, revisiting the nitty gritty and its aftermath, solidifies this understanding.

Tiny Farm Duluth has proven its viability as a business. Between that and my wife's increasing reach as an artist, our family's basic needs are being met. I'm finally free to write without pressure of pen reaping an income. I'm following the advice I gave Shawna early on. "Paint whatever lights you up. Don't worry about the money. Anything you might earn at this point won't significantly alter our lives. Place the long term above short-term concerns…"

But, we aren't comfortable. This is creativity's sweet spot. The pandemic forced severe constraints upon my writing time. In a continuing theme, the problem became the solution.

Constraints and limitations have long been key to any success I've had. I'm unusually gifted at making the most of whatever meager assets we have on hand. Give me something small and humble, and I uncover beauty. Grant me endless space to create, and this mysterious alchemy disappears. I'll never understand why this is. So, with writing, day after day strung together with copious amounts of time results in a big pile of nothing. It's as if I become drunk on all that time, as incoherent thoughts bump around in my skull.

The pandemic and distance learning changed all that. Four of us were in this small house together all the time. Further complicating things, my son required this computer for school every day. If I was going to accomplish any writing at all, it would be before dawn. Day after day I arose at 4 am without an alarm clock, excited to get going. Today, for example, I started out by brewing the coffee, soaked several thousand grams of pea seed for later planting, and will bang out 1500 words before Joey commandeers this station at 9 am. These constraints made me reliably productive for the first time.

I arrived at the solution. I could never have willed myself here. The long, arduous struggle was essential for reaching this point. I nearly added the word arrived, but this wouldn't be true. I'm still a somewhat mediocre writer, but I have promise. Writing makes me come alive and is one of my reasons for being here at this moment in history. Understanding and accepting this has been revolutionary to my entire existence. This is no longer some vague dream. I'm living it right now.

The act of writing amplifies the beauty of the farm business, and the incredible flexibility it affords me. I could never become the writer I'm meant to be while working a full-time job. While most farmers fund their farming habit through employment, the farm business is funding my writing. Oh, how freeing this is! It only took seven years to reach this place, but we're finally here. I hold loosely to the arrangement, knowing forces outside my control could alter this delicate balance. For now, this is a risk worth taking.

I'm no longer committing an absurd amount of money while calculating a future return on investment. The quest transformed into securing a lifestyle that suits us. We doubled down on a life that we might not need to retire from. I write in the morning, enjoy coffee-talk with my wife after she wakes up, and then head out to the spacious sunroom for planting duties and such. It's a splendid connection of brain and body that I've always needed. I'm grateful to have stumbled into this, or, perhaps more accurately, been led into it.

45

Our relationship with money will never be the same. Contrary to years of direct deposit-entitlement inside Cubicle Land's light-deprived depths, our income's significance transcends trifling dollars and cents. Life-sustaining revenue is a consequence of our labor: what we've grown, made with our hands, created, and poured ourselves into. Payments arrive from individuals and businesses who value the fruit of our work. The contrast to being a cog buried in a corporate machine, trading time for cash, is like passing into another dimension.

Every coin sinking into the larder is meaningful—similar to those months with the puppy jar—and fills us with gratitude. When a friend handed me a $10 bill for microgreens, for example, I excitedly told him that Alexander would assist us on our family's first cross-country trek through the Smoky Mountains. Perhaps he'd make it all the way to the ocean with us.

Alas, it wasn't meant to be. An hour later, Mr. Hamilton

joined a bundle of cash remitted to the dog groomer. The money was quickly recycled a half-mile from home.

The next day, 22 hours prior to departure, Shawna received an order on her website for over $2000 in original paintings. In 2018, it was the largest internet order we had ever seen. A sale like that was a month of living expenses. This time, it paid for our entire vacation.

Income flows in and out of our household with intentionality and gratitude now. We understand how much life energy goes into it, and yet we are just stewards of these resources. There's a greater surety that the money flowing in is being entrusted to us for wise use, and not to be possessed.

This sense of money flowing into our well, akin to water from an inexhaustible aquifer, has revolutionized my relationship with finances. It is a renewable resource. We can always sell more art, microgreens, and maybe even an armload of books. Oddly enough, major expenses like our new metal roof, after a complete reinforcement of the underlying structure that was failing after 110 years of faithful service, become opportunities for thanksgiving.

The roof would have collapsed during this winter's record-breaking snowfall if it weren't for the diligence of my carpenter (now a good friend). Instead, the weight just slides right off.

We have many lines in the water; a family of ice fisherman always punching fresh holes through the ice. Shawna's paintings are on display at several galleries throughout our region, and another in Palm Springs, way out in the Golden State. An exhibition space on the opposite coast went out of business during the pandemic, a reminder that we cannot become overly dependent upon a single outlet. Expensive art doesn't fly off the walls, or from shawnagilmore.com. She has created enough assets, however, that connoisseurs of whimsical beauty stumble upon the perfect piece at the right moment in their lives at regular intervals.

I currently have 25 outstanding invoices at grocery stores and restaurants, along with three harvests of microgreens emerging at all stages in the pipeline. My feeble efforts at writing this very sentence might one day produce a few shekels following your purchase. Thank you!

We aren't wholly reliant on any one thing, nor are we overly confident in our abilities. This is a dance between trust in future provision and simultaneously striving to best use the talents we're stewarding.

Reaching this point in the journey has been a struggle. My kids had reached the exact midpoint of childhood when I was laid off. Tradeoffs were profound. Existential, in fact. Sacrifice, patience, and persistence have paid off, but they were painful. It meant incurring zero bad debt, no impulse purchases whatsoever, and the aforementioned ability to say no to our kids, which was exhausting. They had to learn contentment for the fulfilling of needs, even as many wants went unmet. I believe this may prove beneficial to their long-term development, but only time will tell.

We live on the wealthier side of town. Many classmates in the public school have enjoyed extravagant spring break trips every year of their lives. Our kids, who easily qualify for free lunch, were treated to smaller, low-key jaunts to regional destinations. Two vacations over their entire lives veered into exotic territory, the most recent being a remote corner of Montana where we enjoyed horses for neighbors amidst a backdrop of mountains.

The Beartooth Pass was otherworldly, as was the daylong drive book-ending it across some of our nation's finest terrain, but it wasn't the highlight. Peak satisfaction came with melding seamlessly into the awe-inspiring landscape, stillness so complete that we became objects in a painting. Our fleet of hammocks logged dozens of hours beside the Stillwater River. A world-class trout stream, I was incapable of untangling the reel of the Shakespeare fly rod enthusiastically purchased as a boy after watching A River Runs Through It, or of justifying the liquidation of hundreds of dollars from our savings for out-of-state licenses.

Effortless relaxation is always an option, even on vacation.

With an engaging book propped on my chest, every so often I glanced at the kid beside me, equally enthralled in their choice of reads. Companionable silence was the pinnacle, our favorite recreational sport.

A rare week away, I wish we could have enjoyed more trips like this. It was all we could do.

While working through this chapter's first draft, a conversation with a friend about their kids' many activities (traveling to games, etc) sent me into a two-day depression, as I worked through our alternative reality. Instead of multiple sports, our kids have spent the past couple of years working part-time jobs, relieving pressure from our finances as they shoulder some of their own burden.

In darker moments, I've borne a sense of guilt in observing other parents admirably sacrifice vocational fulfillment and spare time so they can provide better lives for their children. Unlike them, we haven't always been able to place kids at the very center of our attention, although we have always been available. Thankfully, in their senior year of high school, I've finally rested in our choices. The angst is gone.

Which path is better? The answer might not be the same for every family.

Yesterday, on the last Sunday of April, I passed a stadium filling with families and athletes at 9:00 on a dimly lit morning. It was 39 degrees, windy, and damp. I was happy to not be among them, cheering on a game involving sticks and balls and running back and forth. Once upon a time, we were out there with them. In that world, the gravitational pull placing children at the center of existence is almost impossible to resist.

I've watched my parents flounder in work for decades that failed to express or develop any innate giftedness. This journey has been an alternative gift. Our kids have witnessed our sense of fulfillment flower as we've muddled along, slowly growing our abilities in service to the world.

Living through the business startup phase with a family was more difficult than I ever imagined. My wish for you, if there is any interest in pursuing something alternative, is that you'd build something on the side long before it's expected to sustain life.

As for us, The Struggle was essential for passing through mystery, a kind of skeleton key.

46

Today marks a full year inside my new grow space. The south-facing wall is primarily glass. In winter months, the sun's low angle streams in directly, infusing my crops and spirit. Ironically, the plants receive less natural light around the summer solstice, since the heliosphere is high overhead. This is a gift, because heat would otherwise become unmanageable. The room is a kind of sundial, imprinting daily and hourly awareness of its arc across the horizon.

With racks set against the wall, east to west and floor-to-ceiling, this is indoor verticalized agriculture. It's hardly the acreage of my dreams, but a wall of greens, reds, and purples has its beauty.

An array of lights, 168 linear feet of LED's in total, illuminate tender foliage. The intensity of all the lights coming on at once is quite brilliant. Though essentially an indoor business, I require constant outdoor access and influence. Obviously, this is why I went into farming in the first place!

Large windows on three sides create a fishbowl effect, lighting up the yard like Clark Griswold's Christmas display. I rush to close the shades before enemy satellites identify this location as a first-strike priority. The roof extends across an adjoining porch where I sow seed. Records spin on the turntable, filling the room with music that spills out the open door to my planting table outside, where sometimes its raining or snowing. The only real obstacles to working out there are high winds and bitter cold. Even then, I step outside to fill my lungs with fresh air and take in the scene.

The most unglamorous task involves scrubbing 70 trays after the harvest. I'm tired after cutting, packing, and delivering, but this giant stack needs to be cleaned in the large stainless steel sink with a scrub brush. One at a time, get 'er done. This week the sun was setting in glory to the west, so I waited to draw the shades as the pinkish sky darkened to red, and finally black (all by 5 pm in late November). First Aid Kit's latest album was playing, and I discovered that this previously hated task had become an act of worship. My spirit soared. The sky's beauty washed through the open windows, and my work was similarly on full display outside. What was previously hidden is now visible. Developing this space has become the capstone for crafting a life that emotes spontaneous worship, gratitude, and joy.

Bustling microgreen operations commonly exist within large, windowless warehouses, but a plant factory wouldn't move my spirit. The automaton-like work would fail to bring me joy, becoming just another job performed solely for cash. In committing to this sunroom, I've obligated myself to keeping Tiny Farm Duluth small. I'll need to uncover more efficient ways of using available space if growth becomes a priority.

Hiring an employee would be nice, but I'd have to triple the size of the business, needlessly complicating our lives. At the current state, sized to meet the needs of a minimum viable audience, we ride out ebbs and flows in demand without undue stress.

Leaving the grow space, we pass through a pair of French doors, where I now sit and write, just 15 feet away. Fifteen feet to the north, in near perfect symmetry, rests my wife's art studio. This is a true three-legged stool. Each business depends on the others, and overlap into our lives. Work and life are almost indistinguishable. All three—art, farm, writing—are things people pine after in futility for a lifetime. Instead of waiting for ideal circumstances, such as being picked by gatekeepers or an unexpected inheritance funding the purchase of land, it is possible to do what you love right now. Not tomorrow.

Today.

Becoming rooted locally, as described in that deepest longing to my Mayor, required building a sustainable lifestyle. This has meant producing within the intersection of talents and resources, and the community's willingness to pay. By being lit up, expressing innate creativity and passion, I'm finally capable of producing something of tangible value for my neighbors. The same goes for Shawna, and hopefully my kids long before they reach their 40's.

Pure joy and love, directed horizontally and vertically, is the secret sauce for vocational fulfillment. Relatively simple as a concept, I've slogged through decades to finally get it. Sort of. It's still fleeting, but my, oh my, is it ever worth the chase.

47

The same carpenter who built my grow room reconstructed our roof. Along with help from the Flying Holden boys, they left gleaming steel in their wake. Andrew, in his 50s, hit the jackpot in hiring these nationally ranked climbers, full of vim and vigor at 18 and 21 years old. Their full humanity burst forth in joyful, chimpanzee-like scaling of scaffolding and ridge, and exuberant willingness to serve. The new covering high in the sky, shiny and radiant, should shed the elements for the rest of my life, a permanent source of gratitude.

I'm not aware of the ultimate cost just yet. Andrew's integrity is unimpeachable. There was no bid. The bill is being paid by our home itself, the equity of which has grown for over a century through world wars and multiple pandemics. Good times and bad.

I like to think that the trinket stamped with my former employer's emblem, a gift, was recycled into these panels of sacred steel. I parted with it a year into the farm's genesis, having waited for the perfect moment. Arriving at the junkyard with a borrowed truck and trailer loaded with metal scrap, a Sanford and Son operation, I parked atop a giant scale as a semi bearing 65,000 pounds waited, engine rumbling. $57 richer, and decked out with a yellow hard hat, I trundled over to a crane-manipulated pile containing thousands of tons of ferrous material. After placing the bright blue, worthless object atop a rusting girder jammed into the jumble, I snapped a photo. The scale of the place, a mere half-mile across open water from touristy shops, commanded the type of reflection typically reserved for a funeral. A less photogenic version of Paddle-to-the-Sea, it sat there until commodity prices reached a certain point, and finally was sent downstream.

That wreckage of a career provided grist for our current lifestyle. We've attained my goal of relative independence. Battling within the bowels of bureaucracy for all those years, constantly hitting my head against a padded cubicle, produced an insatiable longing for connection that propels me.

I pursue it in every interaction, economic and otherwise. It's at root in the exercising of unique gifts in service to others, and particularly in receiving from them. A genuine encounter, even the briefest glimpse of someone's essential essence, elicits joy. Connection's absence, such as an uncaring interaction at a big box store, is a reminder to better seek it out next time.

Way back, in the middle of the beginning of this journey, I received an artist fellowship grant to the tune of $7,000. Underwritten by Minnesota's taxpayers and administered through the Arrowhead Regional Arts Council, the money was directed at funding the creation of a book about living locally. Unfortunately, I wasn't capable of cranking out the work within my specified timeframe—utterly ridiculous—no doubt causing 5.7 million Minnesotans to lean forward in anticipation.

Forging connection with place and people was far more complex than I ever imagined. It required a settling of our family's livelihood. Basic economics, a give-and-take exchange with the community, is an essential driving force. While this work contains the ideas and ideals communicated in my grant proposal, establishing rootedness involves so much more than a basic understanding of local producers. It has required reorienting all of life, and I may never fully arrive. Thank you for your patience.

Epilogue

Dropping our daughter off at college was a whirlwind of triumphs, failures, arguments, confusion, and complex emotions. The life-claiming tornado we encountered—an exclamation mark at the end of a difficult and perplexing day—epitomized the maelstrom. It touched down somewhere to our left as we travelled along the highway, heaving debris 22,000 feet into the sky in the dead of night. Defying gravity, it picked up all this baggage to more politely cross the freeway, passing over dozens of terrified souls who had pulled over inside their metal capsules, praying not to be swallowed up by the unseen behemoth. It touched down some miles to our right, but merely created a swirl of activity above and around us as we screwed in enough courage to go for it. We survived to live another day after rocketing down streets— traffic laws suspended on the edge of an apocalypse—dodging debris clogging every artery.

Compounding anxieties, an offshore criminal organization holds the university's computer systems and internet hostage for what must be an unthinkable ransom, cluttering and complicating the lives of tens of thousands of bright-eyed students eager to begin new chapters in one of the most prestigious institutions in all the world. Doubts infiltrate the fortress.

Regret?

While we were two states and three Great Lakes away, I received a request to consult with a group that could potentially render my little business obsolete. After pausing a while and inquiring, for I admire the leader, I chose to sit out an opportunity to train in those who might replace me with such deep pockets. I'm not immune to the old scarcity mindset. Here I sit in faith, doing work to the best of my ability as a farmer/writer, though I have no assurance of success, or that we'll be fortunate enough to continue in this way of being even a year from now, let alone until our deaths. This uncertainty—fears and doubts that emerge from out of nowhere—beckon me to continue striving with these God-given gifts to the best of my ability, holding on to love and joy, full steam ahead. Damn the torpedoes!

Meanwhile, our son has chosen a simpler path to navigate. He's knee-deep in a welding program at a community college. Living at home, his expenses are minimal. School is manageable, though he also works 30 hours a week and commits at least that much time to learning how to fish, a level of devotion and focus that I find mystifying.

Joey settled into welding after stumbling into a three-day welding camp just this past spring, during his senior year of high school, demonstrating just how little of his future rests upon my slender shoulders. His interests and gifting surely didn't spring from anything I've consciously imparted, and the vocational choice seems incredibly ironic after reflecting upon my awe in the usefulness wielded by the fella driving the "Welders on Wheels" truck way back near the beginning of this journey.

And my wife, who has worked so hard with that daughter who now lives so far away, processing feelings and situations while training her to navigate this wild, unpredictable world, is the most incredible parent to whom I've borne witness. Naturally, she'll be the main point of contact for this adult child hybrid. My feelings during this transition aren't of jealousy, for her closeness was hard-earned. Where is my place in the years ahead?

Have we done everything right?

Have we done anything right?

Have I been rendered redundant, like some insect whose only purpose was to pass on his genetic material and now must wait around to die?

I don't think so.

All this, every complicated bit and so much more, is an opportunity to exercise faith in this being I claim has dominion over the entire universe, and then some, urging me to draw near in friendship to this One who calls us toward greater communion, understanding, and joy, particularly when we do not know what lies ahead. Not only is this the way out of the cubicle, it is the key to everything.

In Gratitude

I recently rolled up my sleeves en route to scrubbing 70 dirty microgreen trays, a spectacular opportunity for listening to Stephen King's sixth installment of the Dark Tower series. At the moment I brought the scrub brush down on that first tray, the author quoted Leif Enger. I was gobsmacked! Happily for me, I have something Stephen does not: Leif's friendship. He took the time to read this book's manuscript when it was still a hot mess, provided valuable feedback, and somehow had the gumption to read the final draft a couple years later, prompting me to tack on the epilogue for a more satisfying ending. I couldn't implement all of his advice, because I am a ham-fisted surgeon. Once I've sewn up a patient, re-opening the wound becomes far too intricate for my skill level.

Dani Westholm also provided invaluable criticism, and then had the gall to pay for lunch when we met to discuss this project. The English teacher from the Cornucopia chapter, her unabashed love and enthusiasm for literature and students only grows with time. I would be a much better reader and writer today if I had come of age with a mentor like her. Westholm's impact on the world, an irresistible consequence of unrestrained joy, is incalculable. Dani, thank you for making this once-in-a-lifetime investment in my life.

These jewels of humanity were indispensable in crafting and pressing on to finish this book, and thus were foundational to supporting my life's work and happiness. I failed to deliver on half of their suggestions. Hopefully, this imperfect attempt will suffice.

I was incapable of carrying this book into the world by myself. After attempting to wield software with a feeble mind, and cresting the rim of depression, I turned to Naomi Christenson. She provided all the graphic design work, and many necessary details that drain life right out of me. Naomi, thanks for bringing Spock into this project and for not being a quitter!

My wife, Shawna Gilmore, captured the essence of this book by painting the cover image. We were perplexed for months, but waited patiently for her mysterious powers to coalesce. She arrived at this idea an hour after some incredible stress blew away, forever reminding me why we've made so many choices that bring us into greater simplicity.

This activity is made possible in part by the voters of Minnesota through a grant from the Arrowhead Regional Arts Council, thanks to a legislative appropriation from the arts and cultural heritage fund.

**Sign up for my email list at
EddyGilmore.com**
to learn of new books when they're fresh out of the oven. It
means the world to me, as would a review. Thanks!

Also by Eddy Gilmore

The Emancipation of a Buried Man
Available at EddyGilmore.com

Made in the USA
Monee, IL
14 November 2023

46550604R00162